RICHARD LOVELACE

Selected Poems

Edited with an Introduction
and Notes by
GERALD HAMMOND

GW00649208

Fyfield*Books*

To Fayaz and Maryam

First published in Great Britain 1987 by
Carcanet Press Limited
208-212 Corn Exchange Buildings
Manchester M4 3BQ

and 198 Sixth Avenue, New York
NY 10013

British Library Cataloguing in Publication Data

Lovelace, Richard
  Selected poems.
  I. Title   II. Hammond, Gerald
  821'.4   PR3542.L2

  ISBN 0-85635-673-5

The publisher acknowledges financial assistance
from the Arts Council of Great Britain

Typeset in 10pt Palatino by Bryan Williamson, Manchester
Printed in England by SRP Ltd, Exeter

Contents

5

Introduction

Andrew Marvell wrote only two poems in commendation of the work of fellow poets. One was for *Paradise Lost*. The other, some twenty years earlier, was for Richard Lovelace's first volume of poems, *Lucasta*, in 1649. They were both, in their way, as much political as artistic statements. The old, blind poet hailed in the later poem had narrowly avoided the wrath of the restored Stuart monarchy. The cavalier whom Marvell defends so vigorously in the first was in prison, with his property sequestered by a parliament which saw him as a political enemy. Marvell's is the only one of the commendatory poems to *Lucasta* which addresses the matter of the authorities' refusal to allow the volume to be published: the Stationer's Register records that it was licensed on 4 February 1648, but it was not actually published until 14 May 1649. After lamenting the degeneration of the times to the point that he now sees 'the envious caterpillar sit / On the fair blossom of each growing wit', Marvell expands the insect image to describe the siege which the imprisoned Lovelace is undergoing:

> The air's already tainted with the swarms
> Of insects which against you rise in arms.
> Word-peckers, paper-rats, book-scorpions,
> Of wit corrupted, the unfashioned sons.
> The barbed censurers begin to look
> Like the grim consistory on thy book;
> And on each line cast a reforming eye,
> Severer than the young Presbytery.
>
> Till when in vain they have thee all perused,
> You shall for being faultless be accused.
> Some reading your *Lucasta*, will allege
> You wronged in her the House's privilege.
> Some that you under sequestration are,
> Because you write when going to the war,

7

> And one the book prohibits, because Kent
> Their first petition by the author sent.

In the couplet which rounds off this list of speculations about the authorities' motives, Marvell has gone back seven years, to the very beginnings of the civil war. S.R. Gardner, whose history of those times is still authoritative, thought that if there were one specific act which led to the outbreak of war, then it was the attempt by Kentish supporters of Charles I to present a loyal petition to parliament, and parliament's suppression of it, having it publicly burned and its organizers imprisoned. These men, led by Sir Edward Dering, were moderate statesmen. With them out of the way their place was filled by younger members of the gentry, who saw this as the opportunity to mobilize the county and march on London, to present the petition in a form and manner which parliament could not resist. At their head was the twenty-four-year-old Richard Lovelace.

In spite of his youth Lovelace had already made a name for himself at court. He had achieved things: an honorary degree from Oxford, a comedy called *The Scholars* which had been presented at Salisbury Court, and military service with Goring's regiment during the two Bishops' wars of 1639-40. But more significant than all of these was the splendid public image which he had created. Anthony Wood, a man not given to excessive hyperbole, had this to say about the young Lovelace:

> ... the most amiable and beautiful person that ever eye beheld, a person also of innate modesty, virtue and courtly deportment, which made him then, but especially after, when he retired to the great city, much admired and adored by the female sex.

But while such images could be cultivated in the 1630s, the next decade put them under a brutal examination. The courtier poets were among the chief casualties. Sir John Suckling took a regiment north in the Bishops' war, all of them decked out in scarlet coats and white doublets. Three years later he committed suicide

8

to avoid his imminent poverty. Edmund Waller tried to put his poetic royalism into practical action by organizing a plot to capture London for the King in 1643. The whole thing went disastrously wrong, and Waller was forced into making the most public and grovelling of apologies to parliament, his name becoming a byword for cowardice. Lovelace's story was not quite so extreme as Suckling's or Waller's, but it bears comparison. Marching at the head of several thousand Kentish men to Blackheath common, he and his fellow leader, Sir William Boteler, were first out-manoeuvred and then put out of commission. Boteler ended up in the Fleet prison, Lovelace in the Gatehouse. The remaining Kentish hotheads were told to go home and behave better in future. By the time Lovelace's petition for release was allowed, in June 1642, the civil war had begun.

Up to this point everything seems to fit Lovelace into the pattern of the archetypal cavalier poet. During this first spell in prison it is quite likely that he had begun to write those definitive accounts of the cavalier experience, whether as a loyal prisoner – 'Stone walls do not a prison make, / Nor iron bars a cage' – or leaving his mistress for the battlefield: 'I could not love thee (dear) so much, / Loved I not honour more.' References to him in the 1640s reinforce our view of him as the ideal poet-lover-soldier which the word *cavalier* epitomizes. John Tatham wrote a poem to him describing him as 'loved Adonis', for whose return Venus can scarcely bear to wait. One of the commendatory poems to *Lucasta* is addressed 'To the Honourable, Valiant, and Ingenious Colonel Richard Lovelace'; and another, by John Hall, asks how so proficient a soldier can be so fine a lover too:

> Was't not enough for us to know how far
> Thou couldst in season suffer, act, and dare?
> But we must also witness with what height
> And what Ionic sweetness thou canst write?
> And melt those eager passions that are
> Stubborn enough t'enrage the god of war,
> Into a noble love...

9

And Marvell's poem moves from its image of the besieged Lovelace, to his rescue by a cavalry charge of ladies, intent on the rescue of their darling:

> But when the beauteous ladies came to know
> That their dear Lovelace was endangered so:
> Lovelace that thawed the most congealed breast,
> He who loved best, and them defended best,
> Whose hand so rudely grasps the steely brand,
> Whose hand so gently melts the ladies' hand,
> They all in mutiny though yet undrest
> Sallied, and would in his defence contest.

The cavalier image was strong enough for the authorities to put Lovelace back in gaol in 1648. While the army was preparing the ground for Charles's execution, there were the beginnings of popular discontent in Kent; and by imprisoning him they were ensuring that at least one of the possible leaders of a revolt was out of action. During this period, late 1648 to early 1649, the publication of *Lucasta* was held up, and Marvell's poem was written. By the time of his second release, Charles was dead and Cromwell's rule assured.

What are we to make of Marvell's defence of Lovelace? After all, within a very short period he would be writing in powerful praise of the Commonwealth – and he is the only major Metaphysical poet who had puritan sympathies. Does the Lovelace poem mark a final stage in his Royalism before the almost exact Charles-Cromwell balance of the 'Horatian Ode'? Or is it an honourable payment of a debt of friendship to a fellow poet now down on his luck? The answer belongs more to a life of Marvell than to an introduction to Lovelace's poems, but the question is worth raising here if only to emphasize the strong links between the two. Marvell is much the more important figure in our view of the seventeenth century and its poetry: critical writing on him outnumbers that on Lovelace by fifty to one. But Lovelace, older by just three years, was a strong influence on Marvell, and not the other way round.

To take the most significant example, there is the long pastoral poem 'Aramantha' (p.52) which brings *Lucasta* to a close. Critics of Marvell's 'Upon Appleton House' only occasionally glance at it, and when they do their purpose is to show how the one poet got it wrong while the other triumphed. James Turner, in *The Politics of Landscape*, compares the two poems, judging that 'despite a considerable resemblance on the surface', Lovelace's poem lacks the control of Marvell's (p.96). All very well, but that recognition of a considerable resemblance ought to be tempered by some acknowledgement of 'Aramantha's' priority. For the reader who has not checked the dates there is no indication of which came first, and no sense that it must have been Marvell's reading of 'Aramantha' in 1649 which introduced him to the idea of a political pastoral, written in octosyllabic couplets, in which the local landscape comes to represent the whole of England, its flora and fauna emerging as types of the factions which fought out the civil war, and which is presided over by an heroine who gradually develops from a vision of arcadian innocence into a complex figure of national and personal salvation. Lovelace does not manage it as subtly as Marvell, but the huge ambition behind this attempt to relate personal to national destiny still makes it one of the most haunting of the mid-century's poems.

When Aramantha tells Alexis that fond (i.e. foolish) man

> to a precipice
> Aspires, till at the top his eyes
> Have lost the safety of the plain,
> Then begs of Fate the vales again

she is summarizing Lovelace's own experiences in the 1640s, and the national experience too. Like many of the poems in this and Lovelace's second volume, 'Aramantha' stands as an imaginative attempt to find ways of comprehending what had happened to turn the world upside down. Its near complete neglect by critics merely demonstrates how partial our view of the century's poetry still is.

11

I do not recommend that the reader begin with 'Aramantha', but reading it between the *Lucasta* poems (pp. 21-62 in this selection) and the *Lucasta. Posthume Poems* volume (pp. 62-94) will reinforce the suspicions which should have begun to form around the earlier lyrics, that Lovelace is a more complete poet than the label *cavalier* would imply, and will help point towards his concern with the nature of his art in the later poems. Its plot is very simple. A rural nymph, Aramantha, encounters a weeping man, Alexis. Alexis, we know from other poems, is Lovelace's name for himself. He is weeping for his supposedly dead Lucasta. Aramantha, after taunting him for his unreasonableness, eventually reveals herself to be Lucasta, and Alexis, overcome with joy, destroys his weapons and retires with her to her pastoral idyll.

In her account of how she came to be exiled into the country Lucasta describes England during the civil war as a state in which both sides, in the name of freedom, destroy

> The glory of this Sicily;
> Since seeking thus the remedy,
> They fancy (building on false ground)
> The means must them and it confound,
> Yet are resolved to stand or fall,
> And win a little or lose all.

This is cruder in statement, but a parallel vision to Marvell's 'Horatian Ode' and 'Appleton House'. The influence Lovelace had upon him was not merely a matter of words and phrases (although it is not difficult to trace these) but one of a lesson in how to be neutral amid 'this sad storm of fire and blood'. Lucasta was doubtless a real person, but she stands for much more than one individual personality – for England itself, and for the poet's muse. 'Aramantha' shows that the way for Lovelace to recover these things is to stand apart from faction: scarcely an attitude which we would expect a true cavalier to take.

Perhaps Lovelace never was the kind of cavalier which Suckling and Waller tried to be, not after the Kentish petition anyway.

The second poem in *Lucasta* is 'To Lucasta, Going to the Wars', and it contains the celebrated cavalier preference for the battle-field over his mistress:

> Tell me not (Sweet) I am unkind,
>   That from the nunnery
> Of thy chaste breast, and quiet mind,
>   To war and arms I fly.

This is the Lovelace which everyone responds to: the effortlessly lyrical statement of elegantly heroic behaviour. It is clever too. Notice how the word *arms* clinches the preference – not her arms, which he runs from, but the soldier's arms, which he runs to. A masculine embrace is superimposed upon a feminine one. But this poem follows directly after 'To Lucasta, Going beyond the Seas', and the ordering of these poems ought to give us pause. They are autobiographically correct. Lovelace did not, as his co-petitioner William Boteler did, stay in England and fight for the King. Instead he went to France and fought in the service of the French king at the siege of Dunkirk. He never, so far as we know, took any part in the civil war, although all of his brothers did. Again, the word *cavalier* seems an odd one to attach to him.

This is not to say that Lovelace never writes cavalier poetry, but he almost never writes the kind of crude and explicit propaganda which other poets of the 1630s and 1640s did. And a poem like 'To Lucasta. From Prison' (p.30) becomes a more subtle composition if we cease to regard it as the product of an unthinking and instinctive Royalist. There Lovelace, after having surveyed the whole country and the degeneration of its institutions, fixes on the king as 'th' only spring / Of all our loves and joys'. But the poem does not end here, and its final three stanzas retreat a little from this certainty of monarchical radiance to a puzzlement at its occlusion, both nationally and in the experience of the man locked away in the prison cell.

> He who being the whole ball
>   Of day on Earth, lends it to all;

When seeking to eclipse his right,
    Blinded, we stand in our own light.

And now an universal mist
    Of error is spread o'er each breast,
With such a fury edged, as is
    Not found in th' inwards of th' abyss.

Oh from thy glorious starry wain
    Dispense on me one sacred beam
To light me where I soon may see
    How to serve you, and you trust me.

This is not a mindless panegyric on Charles, but a sombre attempt to understand how it is possible to serve him properly. What kind of action, or inaction, is now needed? And its inclusiveness is characteristic of Lovelace: the 'we' who 'stand in our own light' are not a 'we' opposed to 'them', but the whole nation. Set it against real cavalier poetry, such as these lines by Thomas Carew, and it becomes clear that Lovelace's is a poetry of a different order.

Then as a father let him be
With numerous issue blest, and see
The fair and godlike offspring grown
From budding stars to suns full blown.
Circle with peaceful olive boughs,
And conquering bays, his regal brows.
Let his strong virtue overcome,
And bring him bloodless trophies home:
Strew all the pavements, where he treads
With loyal hearts, or rebels' heads.
                ('A New-Year's Gift. To the King', 23-32)

All this is not to argue that Lovelace is primarily a political poet – rather, that his poetry includes politics in its general grasp of the mid-century experience. There is, in essence, a coherent poetic personality behind a poem as apparently bizarre and apolitical as 'Lucasta's Fan, With a Looking Glass in it' (p.32), which begins with an apostrophe to an ostrich, and one as obviously political as 'A Fly Caught in a Cobweb' (p.80), which opens with an explicit parallel between the insect and the world's politicians. Between the two stands 'The Grasshopper' (p.28) which poises the political and the apolitical. This is, everyone agrees, a poem about friendship, monarchy, the civil war, the good life, the good man, survival in hard times – it is about grasshoppers too, so that we register both tenor and vehicle when we see the insect who sang through summer reduced to 'green ice' in one of those bitter winters which marked the seventeenth century. In a similar way, the poem about Lucasta's fan encourages us to pay attention to the literal object – and Lovelace writes at his best when he focuses on the impedimenta of polite or impolite life, that is, objects like muffs, shirts, gloves, and glasses of burnt claret – but the perspectives he takes up encourage us to move beyond realism, to the surreal and the symbolic. Here it is relevant to stress his documented interest in the latest achievements of Dutch painting, a super realism which worked in a similar way, making a fly on a cow's flank bigger than a church steeple in the background.

So Lucasta, with her ostrich feather fan winging her side, becomes, for a zany moment, an ostrich herself as she makes her way across the floor

> Sometime they wing her side, then strive to drown
>   The day's eye's-piercing beams, whose am'rous heat
> Solicits still, till with this shield of down
>   From her brave face, his glowing fires are beat.

Such perspectives are typical of Marvell's poetry too, and it is hard to believe that the many odd ways of looking at things which recur throughout *Lucasta* did not encourage him to think of poems as vehicles for visual experimentation. The altered perspectives always have a purpose. A society full of ostriches is one of this poem's concerns, and its final stanza, focusing on the broken fan with its smashed mirror, contains a line of subdued but powerful political comment: 'Now fall'n the brittle favourite lies, and burst'.

15

We can argue that it is all an accident – that the last thing Lovelace intended us to think of was a character like the Duke of Buckingham when he used the phrase 'brittle favourite'. This is certainly how most critics have treated his poetry, but it wilfully ignores the sheer persistence of his oblique approaches to political matters. Consider another poem from early in *Lucasta*, titled simply 'Sonnet'. I have not included it in this selection because there is not room for it. It is simply another reworking of a hackneyed seventeenth-century theme, that it will do no more harm for the lady he courts to share her favours with him than for her to let someone else wear a piece of her jewellery. This is its first stanza:

> Depose your finger of that ring,
>   And crown mine with't awhile;
> Now I restore't – pray does it bring
>   Back with it more of soil?
> Or shines it not as innocent,
>   As honest, as before 'twas lent?

This is undistinguished stuff, and probably quite early. However, it is set quite deliberately in a prominent place in a volume of poems which was licensed at the time when Charles I was under the arrest of his own subjects, and which was published not long after his execution. And there its first three lines wear, with no hint of embarrassment, words which armies had fought over, and would probably do so again: *depose, crown, restore*.

Lovelace's second volume, *Lucasta. Posthume Poems*, contains those poems he probably wrote in the 1650s. As its title indicates, it appeared after his death, under the auspices of his brother Dudley. We do not know exactly when he died, but if Anthony Wood's account is to be believed, his experience through the last few years of his life was one of increasing degradation and despair. The contrast with the dazzling young man who was described as the handsomest man in England in the late 1630s, and who marched on London at the head of the young Kentish gentry could hardly be greater:

After the murder of King Charles I Lovelace was set at liberty, and having by time consumed all his estate, grew very melancholy, (which brought him at length into a consumption) became very poor in body and purse, was the object of charity, went in ragged clothes (whereas when he was in his glory he wore cloth of gold and silver) and mostly lodged in obscure and dirty places, more befitting the worst of beggars, than poorest of servants... He died in a very mean lodging in Gunpowder Alley near Shoe Lane...

C.H. Wilkinson, the editor of the Oxford edition of Lovelace's poetry, poured scorn on this account, and he is generally held to have debunked it sufficiently for it to be considered little better than a piece of fiction. But there is no real reason to distrust Wood. Scholars who have tested his other biographies have found him to be astonishingly reliable, and himself a supporter of the royal cause, there seems little reason for him to have exaggerated Lovelace's misfortunes when members of this loyal family were still alive and helping him by answering his enquiries.

Furthermore, to read the poems of this volume is to move from *Lucasta's* generally court-centred view of English life to a Gunpowder Alley centred one – the buttery rather than the wine cellar, as 'A Loose Saraband' (p.70) has it, where shirts are as tattered as their wearers, and where political struggles are seen in terms of flies trapped in cobwebs. The striking thing is that while Lovelace's poetry grows increasingly personal, it does not become self-indulgent. 'A Fly About a Glass of Burnt Claret' (p.82) is a good example. Watching a fly struggle in the fiery liquor, Lovelace is encouraged to meditate upon his own experience. The fly is a noble lover, hurling himself at a heart of fire which will consume him, and an heroic soldier, sacrificing himself to save his country. He is also entirely insignificant and insanely suicidal. Rescued by the little finger of providence, his instinct is to hurl himself again into the 'moist-hot-glass and liquid fire'. It is all a wonderfully controlled way for Lovelace to look at his own destiny, as victim of the lover-soldier image he had carried into the 1640s.

Lover and soldier, but poet too. The third element makes his *Posthume Poems* so important in the development of seventeenth-century poetry (even if we have so far failed to appreciate this). These poems increasingly emphasize the claim that, more than anything else, he is a professional poet, and that his destiny is bound up with his choice of profession. At times the effect is Yeats-like, as in 'To a Lady with child that asked an Old Shirt' (p.77), where the ragged shirt, all he has to offer, turns out to be the apron from the muse's smock. Of more direct significance is the sense that he stands right at the beginning of Restoration and Augustan satire, with its strong concern with the poet's role. This he explores in a number of poems, and most ambitiously in the final poem in the volume – its equivalent to 'Aramantha' – the splendidly titled 'On Sannazar's being honoured with six hundred ducats by the Clarissimi of Venice, for composing an Elegiac Hexastich of the City. A Satire' (p.86). Here tone, diction and imagery are authentically Dryden's and Pope's. Here is *MacFlecknoe* a generation earlier, in this portrait of the hungry poet eagerly looking forward to a commission to write a poem in celebration of a marriage:

> With what a fury have I known you feed,
> Upon a contract, and the hopes 't might speed;
> Not the fair bride, impatient of delay,
> Doth wish like you the beauties of that day;
> Hotter than all the roasted cooks you sat
> To dress the fricace of your alphabet,
> Which sometimes would be drawn dough anagram,
> Sometimes acrostic parched in the flame;
> Then posies stewed with sippets, mottoes by,
> Of minced verse a miserable pie.   (122-31)

And here is the *Dunciad*, still three generations away, in this picture of the hacks who are beginning to create the Grub Street fraternity:

A mercer now by th' yard does measure o'er
An ode which was but by the foot before;
Deals you an ell of epigram, and swears
It is the strongest and the finest wares.
No wonder if a drawer verses rack,
If 'tis not his 't may be the spir't of sack;
Whilst the fair bar-maid strokes the Muse's teat,
For milk to make the posset up complete.   (212-19)

To have come to this sardonic view of poetry as commodity
from lines like 'I could not love thee (dear) so much / Loved I not
honour more' shows how far Lovelace had travelled through
these two turbulent decades. He lost a lot: his health and property,
and any memorial beyond the poems themselves. He died
obscurely and his grave has disappeared. But the later poems
show no diminution in his achievement, and although Wood's
account of his having grown 'into a melancholy' which led to his
ill health and death may be reflected in the mordancy of some
of his satire, other poems show the same light elegance which
marked the early poems of *Lucasta* – only now they have an edge
of irony to make them even more valuable. Thus the trifle which
he wrote to commend a guide to chess playing (p.86) sums up
the fate of princes, and all other forms of power – court, clergy,
commons – in the simulated perplexity of its couplet: 'Strange,
serious wantoning, all that they / Blustered, and cluttered for,
you play.' So that's what it all meant: a tongue-in-cheek reflection
upon Charles, Strafford, Laud, Pym, and Cromwell, suitably fit-
ting for the friend and mentor of Andrew Marvell.

Textual Note

The spelling has been modernized. Except in a few places I have kept the original punctuation, but most capitals have been reduced to lower-case. References to Wilkinson in the notes are to the single volume Oxford edition of Lovelace's poems, edited by C.H. Wilkinson.

To Lucasta, Going beyond the Seas

If to be absent were to be
    Away from thee;
   Or that when I am gone,
   You or I were alone;
Then my Lucasta might I crave
Pity from blustering wind, or swallowing wave.

But I'll not sigh one blast or gale
    To swell my sail,
   Or pay a tear to suage
   The foaming blue-god's rage;   10
For whether he will let me pass
Or no, I'm still as happy as I was.

Though seas and land betwixt us both,
    Our faith and troth,
   Like separated souls,
   All time and space controls:
Above the highest sphere we meet
Unseen, unknown, and greet as angels greet.

So then we do anticipate
    Our after-fate,   20
   And are alive i' th' skies,
   If thus our lips and eyes
Can speak like spirits unconfined
In heaven, their earthy bodies left behind.

To Lucasta, Going to the Wars

Tell me not (Sweet) I am unkind,
   That from the nunnery
Of thy chaste breast, and quiet mind,
   To war and arms I fly.

True; a new mistress now I chase,
   The first foe in the field;
And with a stronger faith embrace
   A sword, a horse, a shield.

Yet this inconstancy is such,
   As you too shall adore;
I could not love thee (Dear) so much,
   Loved I not honour more.

A Paradox

'Tis true the beauteous star
   To which I first did bow
Burnt quicker, brighter far
   Than that which leads me now;
     Which shines with more delight;
     For gazing on that light
     So long, near lost my sight.

Through foul, we follow fair,
   For had the world one face
And Earth been bright as air,   10
   We had known neither place;
     Indians smell not their nest;
     A Swiss or Finn tastes best,
     The spices of the East.

So from the glorious sun,
   Who to his height hath got,
With what delight we run
   To some black cave, or grot!
      And heavenly Sidney you
      Twice read, had rather view   20
      Some odd Romance, so new.

The god that constant keeps
   Unto his deities,
Is poor in joys, and sleeps
   Imprisoned in the skies:
      This knew the wisest, who
      From Juno stole, below
      To love a bear, or cow.

To Amarantha, That she would dishevel her hair

Amarantha sweet and fair,
Ah braid no more that shining hair!
   As my curious hand or eye,
Hovering round thee let it fly.

Let it fly as unconfined
As its calm ravisher, the wind;
   Who hath left his darling th' East,
To wanton o'er that spicy nest.

Every tress must be confessed
But neatly tangled at the best;   10
   Like a clue of golden thread,
Most excellently ravelléd.

23

Do not then wind up that light
In ribbons, and o'er-cloud in night;
   Like the sun in's early ray,
But shake your head and scatter day.

See 'tis broke! Within this grove
The bower, and the walks of love,
   Weary lie we down and rest,
And fan each other's panting breast.   20

Here we'll strip and cool our fire
In cream below, in milk-baths higher:
   And when all wells are drawn dry,
I'll drink a tear out of thine eye.

Which our very joys shall leave
That sorrows thus we can deceive;
   Or our very sorrows weep,
That joys so ripe, so little keep.

Gratiana dancing and singing

See! with what constant motion
Even, and glorious, as the sun,
   Gratiana steers that noble frame,
Soft as her breast, sweet as her voice
That gave each winding law and poise,
   And swifter than the wings of fame.

She beat the happy pavément
By such a star made firmament,
   Which now no more the roof envies;
But swells up high with Atlas ev'n,   10

Bearing the brighter, nobler heaven,
    And in her, all the deities.

Each step trod out a lover's thought
And the ambitious hopes he brought,
    Chained to her brave feet with such arts,
Such sweet command, and gentle awe,
As when she ceased, we sighing saw
    The floor lay paved with broken hearts.

So did she move; so did she sing
Like the harmonious spheres that bring   20
    Unto their rounds their music's aid;
Which she perforyméd such a way,
As all th' enamoured world will say
    The Graces danced, and Apollo played.

The Scrutiny

Why should you swear I am forsworn,
    Since thine I vowed to be?
Lady it is already morn,
    And 'twas last night I swore to thee
That fond impossibility.

Have I not loved thee much and long,
    A tedious twelve hours' space?
I must all other beauties wrong,
    And rob thee of a new embrace;
Could I still dote upon thy face.   10

Not, but all joy in thy brown hair,
    By others may be found;
But I must search the black and fair
    Like skilful min'ralists that sound
For treasure in unploughed-up ground.

Then, if when I have loved my round,
    Thou prov'st the pleasant she;
With spoils of meaner beauties crowned,
    I laden will return to thee,
    Ev'n sated with variety.   20

A Loose Saraband

Ah me! the little tyrant thief!
    As once my heart was playing,
He snatched it up and flew away,
    Laughing at all my praying.

Proud of his purchase he surveys,
    And curiously sounds it,
And though he sees it full of wounds,
Cruel still on he wounds it.

And now this heart is all his sport,
    Which as a ball he boundeth   10
From hand to breast, from breast to lip,
    And all its rest confoundeth.

Then as a top he sets it up,
    And pitifully whips it;
Sometimes he clothes it gay and fine,
    Then straight again he strips it.

26

He covered it with *false belief*,
   Which gloriously showed it;
And for a morning-cushionet,
   On's mother he bestowed it.   20

Each day with her small brazen stings,
   A thousand times she razed it;
But then at night, bright with her gems,
   Once near her breast she placed it.

There warm it gan to throb and bleed;
   She knew that smart and grievéd;
At length this poor condemnéd heart
   With these rich drugs reprievéd.

She washed the wound with a fresh tear,
   Which my Lucasta droppéd,   30
And in the sleeve-silk of her hair,
   'Twas hard bound up and wrappéd.

She probed it with her constancy,
   And found no rancour nigh it;
Only the anger of her eye,
   Had wrought some proud flesh by it.

Then pressed she nard in every vein
   Which from her kisses trilléd;
And with that balm healed all its pain
   That from her hand distilléd.   40

But yet this heart avoids me still,
   Will not by me be ownéd;
But's fled to its physician's breast,
   There proudly sits enthronéd.

The Grasshopper. To my Noble Friend, Mr Charles Cotton. Ode.

Oh thou that swing'st upon the waving hair
   Of some well-filléd oaten beard,
Drunk every night with a delicious tear
   Dropped thee from heaven, where now th' art reared.

The joys of earth and air are thine entire,
   That with thy feet and wings dost hop and fly;
And when thy poppy works thou dost retire
   To thy carved acorn-bed to lie.

Up with the day, the sun thou welcom'st then,
   Sport'st in the gilt-plaits of his beams,   10
And all these merry days mak'st merry men,
   Thyself, and melancholy streams.

But ah the sickle! Golden ears are cropped;
   Ceres and Bacchus bid good night;
Sharp frosty fingers all your flowers have topped,
   And what scythes spared, winds shave off quite.

Poor verdant fool! and now green ice: thy joys
   Large and as lasting, as thy perch of grass,
Bid us lay in 'gainst winter, rain, and poise
   Their floods, with an o'erflowing glass.   20

Thou best of men and friends! we will create
   A genuine summer in each other's breast;
And spite of this cold time and frozen fate
   Thaw us a warm seat to our rest.

Our sacred hearths shall burn eternally
   As vestal flames, the North-wind, he

Shall strike his frost-stretched wings, dissolve and fly
   This Etna in epitome.

Dropping December shall come weeping in,
   Bewail th' usurping of his reign;   30
But when in showers of old Greek we begin,
   Shall cry, he hath his crown again!

Night as clear Hesper shall our tapers whip
   From the light casements where we play,
And the dark hag from her black mantle strip,
   And stick there everlasting day.

Thus richer than untempted kings are we,
   That asking nothing, nothing need:
Though lord of all what seas embrace; yet he
That wants himself, is poor indeed.   40

The Vintage to the Dungeon

Sing out pent souls, sing cheerfully!
Care shackles you in liberty,
Mirth frees you in captivity:
      Would you double fetters add?
        Else why so sad?
      Chorus
Beside your pinioned arms you'll find
Grief too can manacle the mind.

Live then prisoners uncontrolled;
Drink o' th' strong, the rich, the old,
Till wine too hath your wits in hold;
      Then if still your jollity,
        And throats are free;

Chorus
Triumph in your bonds and pains,
And dance to th' music of your chains.

To Lucasta. From Prison.

Long in thy shackles, liberty,
　I ask not from these walls, but thee;
Left for a while another's bride
　To fancy all the world beside.

Yet ere I do begin to love,
　See! How I all my objects prove;
Then my free soul to that confine,
　'Twere possible I might call mine.

First I would be in love with *Peace*,
　And her rich swelling breasts' increase;   10
But how alas! how may that be,
　Despising Earth, she will love me?

Fain would I be in love with *War*,
　As my dear just avenging star;
But War is loved so everywhere,
　Ev'n he disdains a lodging here.

Thee and thy wounds I would bemoan
　Fair thorough-shot *Religion*;
But he lives only that kills thee,
　And whoso binds thy hands, is free.   20

I would love a *Parliament*
　As a main prop from heaven sent;

30

But ah! Who's he that would be wedded
　　To th' fairest body that's beheaded?

Next would I court my *Liberty*,
　　And then my birth-right, *Property*;
But can that be, when it is known
　　There's nothing you can call your own?

A *Reformation* I would have,
　　As for our griefs a *Sov'reign* salve;　　　　30
That is, a cleansing of each wheel
　　Of State, that yet some rust doth feel:

But not a Reformation so,
　　As to reform were to o'erthrow;
Like watches by unskilful men
　　Disjointed, and set ill again.

The *Public Faith* I would adore,
　　But she is bankrupt of her store;
Nor how to trust her can I see,
For she that cozens all, must me.　　　　　　40

Since then none of these can be
　　Fit objects for my love and me;
What then remains, but th' only spring
　　Of all our loves and joys? The KING.

He who being the whole ball
　　Of day on Earth, lends it to all;
When seeking to eclipse his right,
　　Blinded, we stand in our own light.

And now an universal mist
　　Of error is spread o'er each breast,　　　　50

With such a fury edged, as is
    Not found in th' inwards of th' abyss.

Oh from thy glorious starry wain
    Dispense on me one sacred beam
To light me where I soon may see
    How to serve you, and you trust me.

Lucasta's Fan, With a Looking Glass in it

Ostrich! Thou feathered fool, and easy prey.
    That larger sails to thy broad vessel need'st;
Snakes through thy gutter-neck hiss all the day,
    Then on thy iron mess at supper feed'st.

Oh what a glorious transmigration
    From this, to so divine an edifice
Hast thou straight made! near from a wingéd stone
    Transformed into a bird of paradise!

Now do thy plumes for hue and lustre vie
    With th' arch of heaven that triumphs o'er past wet,   10
And in a rich enamelled pinion lie
    With sapphires, amethysts, and opals set.

Sometime they wing her side, then strive to drown
    The day's eye's-piercing beams, whose am'rous heat
Solicits still, till with this shield of down
    From her brave face, his glowing fires are beat.

But whilst a plumy curtain she doth draw,
    A crystal mirror sparkles in thy breast,
In which her fresh aspect whenas she saw,
    And then her foe retiréd to the west,   20

Dear engine that o' th' sun got'st me the day,
  Spite of his hot assaults mad'st him retreat!
No wind (said she) dare with thee henceforth play
  But mine own breath to cool the tyrant's heat.

My lively shade thou ever shalt retain
  In thy encloséd feather-framéd glass,
And but unto our selves to all remain
  Invisible thou feature of this face!

So said, her sad swain overheard, and cried
  Ye gods! for faith unstained this a reward!   30
Feathers and glass t' outweigh my virtue tried?
  Ah show their empty strength! the gods accord.

Now fall'n the brittle favourite lies, and burst!
  Amazed Lucasta weeps, repents, and flies
To her Alexis, vows herself accursed
  If hence she dress herself, but in his eyes.

Lucasta, taking the waters at Tunbridge

  Ye happy floods! that now must pass
    The sacred conduits of her womb,
  Smooth, and transparent as your face,
    When you are deaf, and winds are dumb.

  Be proud! and if your waters be
    Fouled with a counterfeited tear,
  Or some false sigh hath stainéd ye,
    Haste, and be purifiéd there.

33

And when her rosy gates y' have traced,
    Continue yet some orient wet,   10
Till turned into a gem, y' are placed
    Like diamonds with rubies set.

Ye drops that dew th' Arabian bowers,
    Tell me did you e'er smell or view
On any leaf of all your flowers
    So sweet a scent, so rich a hue?

But as through th' organs of her breath,
    You trickle wantonly, beware;
Ambitious seas in their just death
    As well as lovers must have share.   20

And see! you boil as well as I,
    You that to cool her did aspire,
Now troubled, and neglected lie,
    Nor can yourselves quench your own fire.

Yet still be happy in the thought,
    That in so small a time as this,
Through all the heavens you were brought
    Of Virtue, Honour, Love and Bliss.

To My Worthy Friend Mr Peter Lely: on that excellent Picture of his Majesty, and the Duke of York, drawn by him at Hampton Court

See! what a clouded majesty! and eyes
Whose glory through their mist doth brighter rise!
See! what an humble bravery doth shine,
And grief triumphant breaking through each line!

34

How it commands the face! so sweet a scorn
Never did happy misery adorn!
So sacred a contempt! that others show
To this, (o' th' height of all the wheel) below;
That mightiest monarchs by this shaded book
May copy out their proudest, richest look.   10

    Whilst the true Eaglet this quick lustre spies,
And by his Sun's enlightens his own eyes;
He cares his cares, his burden feels, then straight
Joys that so lightly he can bear such weight;
Whilst either either's passion doth borrow,
And both do grieve the same victorious sorrow.

    These my best Lely with so bold a spirit
And soft a grace, as if thou didst inherit
For that time all their greatness, and didst draw
With those brave eyes your Royal Sitters saw.   20

    Not as of old, when a rough hand did speak
A strong aspect, and a fair face, a weak;
When only a black beard cried villain, and
By hieroglyphics we could understand;
When crystal typified in a white spot,
And the bright ruby was but one red blot;
Thou dost the things orientally the same,
Not only paint'st its colour, but its flame:
Thou sorrow canst design without a tear,
And with the man his very hope or fear;   30
So that th' amazéd world shall henceforth find
None but my Lely ever drew a mind.

Ellinda's Glove

Thou snowy farm with thy five tenements!
    Tell thy white mistress here was one
    That called to pay his daily rents:
But she a gathering flowers and hearts is gone,
And thou left void to rude possession.

But grieve not pretty ermine cabinet,
    Thy alablaster lady will come home;
    If not, what tenant there can fit
The slender turnings of thy narrow room,
But must ejected be by his own doom?

Then give me leave to leave my rent with thee;
    Five kisses, one unto a place:
    For though the lute's too high for me;
Yet servants knowing minikin nor base,
Are still allowed to fiddle with the case.

To Fletcher Revived

How have I been religious? What strange good
Has 'scaped me that I never understood?
Have I hell-guarded heresy o'erthrown?
Healed wounded states? Made kings and kingdoms one?
That Fate should be so merciful to me,
To let me live t' have said I have read thee.

  Fair star ascend! the joy! the life! the light
Of this tempestuous age, this dark world's sight!
Oh from thy crown of glory dart one flame
May strike a sacred reverence, whilst thy name   10

(Like holy flamens to their god of day)
We bowing, sing; and whilst we praise, we pray.

Bright spirit! whose eternal motion
Of wit, like Time, still in itself did run,
Binding all others in it, and did give
Commission, how far this or that shall live;
Like Destiny of poems, who, as she
Signs death to all, herself can never die.

And now thy purple-robéd Tragedy,
In her embroidered buskins, calls mine eye,   20
Where brave Aetius we see betrayed,
T' obey his death, whom thousand lives obeyed;
Whilst that the Mighty Fool his sceptre breaks,
And through his Gen'ral's wounds his own doom speaks,
Weaving thus richly Valentinian
The costliest monarch with the cheapest man.

Soldiers may here to their old glories add,
The lover love, and be with reason mad:
Not as of old, Alcides furious,
Who wilder than his bull did tear the house,   30
(Hurling his language with the canvas stone)
'Twas thought the monster roared the sob'rer tone.

But ah! when thou thy sorrow didst inspire
With passions, black as is her dark attire,
Virgins as sufferers have wept to see
So white a soul, so red a cruelty;
That thou hast grieved, and with unthought redress,
Dried their wet eyes who now thy mercy bless;
Yet loth to lose thy watery jewell, when
Joy wiped it off, laughter straight sprung't again.   40

Now ruddy cheekéd Mirth with rosy wings,
Fans every brow with gladness, whilst she sings
Delight to all, and the whole theatre
A festival in heaven doth appear:
Nothing but pleasure, love, and (like the morn)
Each face a general smiling doth adorn.

Hear ye foul speakers, that pronounce the air
Of stews and shores, I will inform you where
And how to clothe aright your wanton wit,
Without her nasty bawd attending it: 50
View here a loose thought said with such a grace,
Minerva might have spoke in Venus' face;
So well disguised, that 'twas conceived by none
But Cupid had Diana's linen on;
And all his naked parts so veiled, th' express
The shape with clouding the uncomeliness;
That if this Reformation which we
Received, had not been buriéd with thee,
The stage (as this work) might have lived and loved
Her lines, the austere scarlet had approved;   60
And th' actors wisely been from that offence
As clear, as they are now from audience.

Thus with thy genius did the scene expire,
Wanting thy active and correcting fire,
That now (to spread a darkness over all)
Nothing remains but poesie to fall:
And though from these thy embers we receive
Some warmth, so much as may be said, we live,
That we dare praise thee, blushless, in the head
Of the best piece Hermes to Love e'er read,   70
That we rejoice and glory in thy wit,
And feast each other with remembering it,
That we dare speak thy thoughts, thy acts recite;
Yet all men henceforth be afraid to write.

38

Against the Love of Great Ones

Unhappy youth betrayed by Fate
To such a love hath sainted hate,
And damnéd those celestial bands;
Are only knit with equal hands;
The love of great ones? 'Tis a love
Gods are incapable to prove;
For where there is a joy uneven,
There never, never can be heaven:
'Tis such a love as is not sent
To fiends as yet for punishment;   10
Ixion willingly doth feel
The gyre of his eternal wheel,
Nor would he now exchange his pain
For clouds and goddesses again.

Wouldst thou with tempests lie? Then bow
To th' rougher furrows of her brow;
Or make a thunder-bolt thy choice?
Then catch at her more fatal voice;
Or 'gender with the lightning? try
The subtler flashes of her eye: 20
Poor Semele well knew the same,
Who both embraced her god and flame;
And not alone in soul did burn,
But in this love did ashes turn.

How ill doth majesty enjoy
The bow and gaiety o' th' boy,
As if the purple-robe should sit,
And sentence give i' th' chair of wit.

Say ever-dying wretch to whom
Each answer is a certain doom: 30
What is it that you would possess,

The countess, or the naked Bess?
Would you her gown, or title do?
Her box, or gem, her thing or show?
If you mean her, the very her
Abstracted from her character;
Unhappy boy! you may as soon
With fawning wanton with the moon,
Or with an amorous complaint
Get prostitute your very saint;   40
Not that we are not mortal, or
Fly Venus' altars, or abhor
The selfsame knack for which you pine;
But we (defend us!) are divine,
Female, but madam born, and come
From a right-honourable womb:
Shall we then mingle with the base,
And bring a silver-tinsel race?
Whilst th' issue noble will not pass,
The gold allayed (almost half brass)   50
And th' blood in each vein doth appear,
Part thick boorein, part lady clear:
Like to the sordid insects sprung
From Father Sun, and Mother Dung;
Yet lose we not the hold we have,
But faster grasp the trembling slave;
Play at balloon with's heart, and wind
The strings like skeins, steal into his mind
Ten thousand hells, and feignéd joys
Far worse than they, whilst like whipped boys,   60
After this scourge he's hush with toys.

   This heard Sir, play still in her eyes,
And be a dying lives, like flies
Caught by their angle-legs, and whom
The torch laughs piecemeal to consume.

To Althea, From Prison

When Love with unconfinéd wings
   Hovers within my gates;
And my divine Althea brings
   To whisper at the grates:
When I lie tangled in her hair,
   And fettered to her eye;
The gods that wanton in the air,
   Know no such liberty.

When flowing cups run swiftly round
   With no allaying Thames,   10
Our careless heads with roses bound,
   Our hearts with loyal flames;
When thirsty grief in wine we steep,
   When healths and draughts go free,
Fishes that tipple in the deep,
   Know no such liberty.

When (like committed linnets) I
   With shriller throat shall sing
The sweetness, mercy, majesty,
   And glories of my KING;   20
When I shall voice aloud, how good
   He is, how great should be;
Enlargéd winds that curl the flood,
   Know no such liberty.

Stone walls do not a prison make,
   Nor iron bars a cage;
Minds innocent and quiet take
   That for an hermitage;
If I have freedom in my love,
   And in my soul am free;   30
Angels alone that soar above,
   Enjoy such liberty.

Being Treated, To Ellinda

For cherries plenty, and for corans
Enough for fifty, were there more on's;
For ells of beer, flutes of canary
That well did wash down pasties-mary;
For peason, chickens, sauces high,
Pig, and the widow-ven'son-pie;
With certain promise (to your brother)
Of the virginity of another,
Where it is thought I too may peep in
With knuckles far as any deep in;   10
For glasses, heads, hands, bellies full
Of wine, and loin right-worshipful;
Whether all of, or more behind-a
Thanks freest, freshest, fair Ellinda:
Thanks for my visit not disdaining,
Or at the least thanks for your feigning;
For if your mercy door were locked-well,
I should be justly soundly knocked-well;
Cause that in dog'rell I did mutter
Not one rhyme to you from dam-Rotter.   20

Next beg I to present my duty
To pregnant sister in prime beauty,
Whom well I deem (e'er few months elder)
Will take out Hans from pretty Kelder,
And to the sweetly fair Mabella,
A match that vies with Arabella;
In each respect but the misfortune,
Fortune, Fate, I thee importune.

Nor must I pass the lovely Alice,
Whose health I'd quaff in golden chalice;   30
But since that Fate hath made me neuter,
I only can in beaker pewter:

42

But who'd forget, or yet left unsung
The doughty acts of George the young-son?
Who yesterday to save his sister
Had slain the snake, had he not missed her:
But I shall leave him till a nag on
He gets to prosecute the dragon;
And with the help of sun and taper,
Fill with his deeds twelve reams of paper,   40
That Amadis, Sir Guy and Topaz
With his fleet neigher shall keep no-pace.
    But now to close all I must switch-hard,
    Servant ever;
                 Lovelace Richard.

A Guiltless Lady Imprisoned; after penanced

Hark fair one how whate'er here is
    Doth laugh and sing at thy distress;
Not out of hate to thy relief,
    But joy t' enjoy thee, though in grief.

See! that which chains you, you chain here;
    The prison is thy prisoner;
How much thy gaoler's keeper art,
    He binds your hands, but you his heart.

The gyves to raze so smooth a skin,
    Are so unto themselves within,   10
But blest to kiss so fair an arm
    Haste to be happy with that harm.

And play about thy wanton wrist
    As if in them thou so wert dressed;

43

But if too rough, too hard they press,
  Oh they but closely, closely kiss.

And as thy bare feet bless the way
  The people do not mock, but pray,
And call thee as amazed they run
  Instead of prostitute, a nun.   20

The merry torch burns with desire
  To kindle the eternal fire,
And lightly dances in thine eyes
  To tunes of epithalamies.

The sheets tied ever to thy waist,
  How thankful to be so embraced!
And see! thy very very bands
  Are bound to thee, to bind such hands.

To his Dear Brother Colonel F.L.
Immoderately Mourning my Brother's Untimely
Death at Carmarthen

If tears could wash the ill away,
A pearl for each wet bead I'd pay;
But as dewed corn the fuller grows,
So watered eyes but swell our woes.

One drop another calls, which still
(Grief adding fuel) doth distill;
Too fruitful of herself is anguish,
We need no cherishing to languish.

44

Coward Fate degen'rate Man
Like little children uses, when   10
He whips us first until we weep,
Then 'cause we still a weeping keep.

Then from thy firm self never swerve;
Tears fat the grief that they should starve;
Iron decrees of destiny
Are ne'er wiped out with a wet eye.

But this way you may gain the field,
Oppose but sorrow and 'twill yield;
One gallant thorough-made resolve
Doth starry influence dissolve.   20

La Bella Bona Roba

I cannot tell who loves the skeleton
Of a poor marmoset, nought but bone, bone.
Give me a nakedness with her clothes on.

Such whose white-satin upper coat of skin,
Cut upon velvet rich incarnadine,
Has yet a body (and of flesh) within.

Sure it is mean husbandry in men,
Who do incorporate with aery lean,
T' repair their sides, and get their rib again.

Hard hap unto that huntsman that decrees
Fat joys for all his sweat, whenas he sees,
After his 'say, nought but his keeper's fees.

45

Then Love I beg, when next thou tak'st thy bow,
Thy angry shafts, and dost heart-searching go,
Pass rascal deer, strike me the largest doe.

The Fair Beggar

Commanding asker, if it be
   Pity that you fain would have,
Then I turn beggar unto thee,
   And ask the thing that thou dost crave;
I will suffice thy hungry need
So thou wilt but my fancy feed.

In all ill years, was't ever known
   On so much beauty such a dearth?
Which in that thrice-bequeathéd gown
   Looks like the sun eclipsed with earth,   10
Like gold in canvas, or with dirt
Unsoiléd ermines close begirt.

Yet happy he that can but taste
   This whiter skin who thirsty is,
Fools dote on satin motions laced,
   The gods go naked in their bliss,
At th' barrel's head there shines the vine,
There only relishes the wine.

There quench my heat, and thou shalt sup
   Worthy the lips that it must touch: 20
NECTAR from out the starry cup,
   I beg thy breath not half so much;
So both our wants supplied shall be,
You'll give for love, I charity.

Cheap then are pearl-embroideries
    That not adorn, but clouds thy waist;
Thou shalt be clothed above all price,
    If thou wilt promise me embraced;
We'll ransack neither chest or shelf,
I'll cover thee with mine own self.   30

But Cruel, if thou dost deny
    This necessary alms to me;
What soft-souled man but with his eye
    And hand will hence be shut to thee?
Since all must judge you more unkind;
I starve your body, you my mind.

Amyntor from beyond the Sea to Alexis. A Dialogue.

Amyntor
Alexis! ah Alexis! can it be
    Though so much wet and dry
      Doth drown our eye,
Thou keep'st thy wingéd voice from me?

Alexis
Amyntor a profounder sea I fear
    Hath swallowed me, where now
      My arms do row,
I float i' th' ocean of a tear.

Lucasta weeps lest I look back and tread
    Your watery land again.   10
Amyntor I'd through the rain,
    Such showers are quickly over-spread.

47

Conceive how joy after this short divorce
        Will circle her with beams,
                When like your streams
        You shall roll back with kinder force

And call the helping winds to vent your thought.
Alex. Amyntor! Chloris where,
                Or in what sphere
        Say may that glorious fair be sought?   20

                Amyntor
She's near the centre of these arms o'er blest
                Whence may she never move
                        Till Time and Love
                Haste to their everlasting rest.

                Alexis
Ah subtle swain! doth not my flame rise high
                As yours, and burn as hot?
                        Am not I shot
                With the self same artillery?

And can I breathe without her air? *Amyn.* Why then
                From thy tempestuous Earth   30
                        Where blood and dearth
                Reign 'stead of kings, again

Waft thyself over, and lest storms from far
                Arise, bring in our sight
                        The sea's delight,
                Lucasta that bright Northern star.

                Alexis
But as we cut the rugged deep, I fear
                The green-god stops his fell
                        Chariot of shell
                And smoothes the main to ravish her.   40

Amyntor

Oh no, the Prince of waters' fires are done,
    He as his empire old
      And rivers cold,
His queen now runs abed to th' sun;

But all his treasure he shall ope that day:
    Tritons shall sound, his fleet
      In silver meet,
And to her their rich offerings pay.

Alexis

We fly Amyntor, not amazed how sent
    By water, earth, or air: 50
      Or if with her
      By fire, ev'n there
I move in mine own element.

A Lady with a Falcon on her fist. To the Honourable my Cousin A.L.

This queen of prey (now prey to you)
    Fast to that perch of ivory
In silver chains and silken clue
    Hath now made full thy victory:

The swelling Admiral of the dread
    Cold deep, burnt in thy flames, Oh Fair!
Was't not enough, but thou must lead
    Bound too the princess of the air?

Unarmed of wings and scaly oar,
    Unhappy crawler on the land,   10

To what heav'n fli'st? div'st to what shore
    That her brave eyes do not command?

Ascend the chariot of the sun
    From her bright pow'r to shelter thee:
Her captive (fool) outgazes him;
    Ah what lost wretches then are we!

Now proud usurpers on the right
    Of sacred beauty hear your doom;
Recant your SEX, your MAST'RY, MIGHT;
    Lower you cannot be o'ercome: 20

Repent ye e'er named HE or HEAD,
    For y' are in Falcon's monarchy,
And in that just dominion bred
    In which the NOBLER is the SHE.

Calling Lucasta from her Retirement. Ode.

From the dire monument of thy black room
Where now that vestal flame thou dost entomb
As in the inmost cell of all Earth's womb,

Sacred Lucasta like the pow'rful ray
Of Heavenly Truth pass this Cimmerian way,
Whilst all the standards of your beams display:

Arise and climb our whitest highest hill,
There your sad thoughts with joy and wonder fill,
And see seas calm as Earth, Earth as your will.

Behold how lightning like a taper flies   10
And gilds your chari't, but ashaméd dies
Seeing itself out-gloried by your eyes.

Threat'ning and boistrous tempests gently bow,
And to your steps part in soft paths, when now
There nowhere hangs a cloud, but on your brow.

No show'rs but 'twixt your lids, nor gelid snow,
But what your whiter chaster breast doth owe,
Whilst winds in chains colder your sorrow blow.

Shrill trumpets now do only sound to eat,
Artillery hath loaden every dish with meat,   20
And drums at every health alarms beat.

All things LUCASTA, but LUCASTA call,
Trees borrow tongues, waters in accents fall,
The air doth sing, and fire's musical.

Awake from the dead vault in which you dwell,
All's loyal here, except your thoughts rebel,
Which so let loose, often their gen'ral quell.

See! She obeys! by all obeyéd thus;
No storms, heats, colds, no souls contentious,
Nor civil war is found – I mean, to us.   30

Lovers and angels, though in heaven they show
And see the woes and discords here below,
What they not feel, must not be said to know.

Aramantha. A Pastoral.

Up with the jolly bird of light
Who sounds his third retreat to Night;
Fair Aramantha from her bed
Ashaméd starts, and rises red
As the carnation-mantled Morn,
Who now the blushing robe doth spurn,
And puts on angry grey, whilst she
The envy of a deity
Arrays her limbs, too rich indeed
To be enshrined in such a weed;   10
Yet lovely 'twas and strait, but fit;
Not made for her, but she to it:
By nature it sat close and free,
As the just bark unto the tree:
Unlike love's martyrs of the town,
All day imprisoned in a gown,
Who racked in silk 'stead of a dress,
Are clothéd in a frame or press,
And with that liberty and room,
The dead expatiate in a tomb.   20

   No cabinets with curious washes,
Bladders, and perfuméd plashes;
No venom-tempered water's here,
Mercury is banishéd this sphere:
Her pail's all this, in which wet glass,
She both doth cleanse and view her face.

   Far hence all Iberian smells,
Hot amulets, pomander spells;
Fragrant gales, cool air, the fresh,
And natural odour of her flesh,   30
Proclaim her sweet from th' womb as morn.
Those coloured things were made not born,
Which fixed within their narrow straights,
Do look like their own counterfeits.

So like the Provence Rose she walked,
Flowered with blush, with verdure stalked;
Th' officious wind her loose hair curls,
The dew her happy linen pearls,
But wets a tress, which instantly
Sol with a crisping beam doth dry.   40
   Into the garden is she come,
Love and Delight's Elysium;
If ever Earth showed all her store,
View her discoloured budding floor;
Here her glad eye she largely feeds,
And stands 'mongst them, as they 'mong weeds;
The flowers in their best array,
As to their queen their tribute pay,
And freely to her lap proscribe
A daughter out of every tribe: 50
Thus as she moves, they all bequeath
At once the incense of their breath.
   The noble Heliotropian
Now turns to her, and knows no sun;
   And as her glorious face doth vary,
So opens loyal golden Mary;
Who if but glancéd from her sight,
Straight shuts again as it were night.
   The Violet (else lost i' th' heap)
Doth spread fresh purple for each step;   60
With whose humility possessed,
Sh' enthrones the poor Girl in her breast:
The July-flower that hereto thrived,
Knowing herself no longer lived,
But for one look of her, upheaves,
Then 'stead of tears straight sheds her leaves.
   Now the rich robéd Tulip, who
Clad all in tissue close doth woo,
Her (sweet to th' eye but smelling sour)
She gathers to adorn her bower.   70

But the proud Honeysuckle spreads
Like a pavilion her heads,
Contemns the wanting commonalty,
That but to two ends useful be,
And to her lips thus aptly placed,
With smell and hue presents her taste.

So all their due obedience pay,
Each thronging to be in her way:
Fair Aramantha with her eye
Thanks those that live, which else would die: 80
The rest in silken fetters bound,
By crowning her are crown and crowned.

And now the sun doth higher rise,
Our Flora to the meadow hies:
The poor distresséd heifers low,
And as sh' approacheth gently bow,
Begging her charitable leisure
To strip them of their milky treasure.

Out of the yeomanry o' th' herd,
With grave aspect, and feet prepared,   90
A rev'rend lady cow draws near,
Bids Aramantha welcome here;
And from her privy purse lets fall
A pearl or two, which seem to call
This adorned adoréd fairy
To the banquet of her dairy.

Soft Aramantha weeps to see
'Mongst men such inhumanity
That those who do receive in hay,
And pay in silver twice a day,   100
Should by their cruel barb'rous theft,
Be both of that, and life bereft.

But 'tis decreed whene'er this dies,
That she shall fall a sacrifice
Unto the gods, since those that trace
Her stem, show 'tis a god-like race;

Descending in an even line
From heifers, and from steers divine,
Making the honoured extract full
In Io and Europa's bull.   110
She was the largest goodliest beast,
That ever mead or altar blest;
Round as her udder, and more white
Than is the milky way in night:
Her full broad eye did sparkle fire,
Her breath was sweet as kind desire,
And in her beauteous crescent shone,
Bright as the argent-hornéd moon.

But see! this whiteness is obscure,
Cynthia spotted, she impure;   120
Her body writhelled, and her eyes
Departing lights at obsequies:
Her lowing hot, to the fresh gale,
Her breath perfumes the field withal;
To those two suns that ever shine,
To those plump parts she doth enshrine,
To th' hovering snow of either hand,
That Love and Cruelty command.

After the breakfast on her teat,
She takes her leave o' th' mournful neat,   130
Who by her touched now prize their life,
Worthy alone the hollowed knife.

Into the neighb'ring wood she's gone,
Whose roof defies the tell-tale sun,
And locks out every prying beam;
Close by the lips of a clear stream
She sits and entertains her eye
With the moist crystal, and the fry
With burnished-silver mailed, whose oars
Amazéd still make to the shores;   140
What need she other bait or charm
But look? or angle, but her arm?

The happy captive gladly ta'n,
Sues ever to be slave in vain,
Who instantly (confirmed in's fears)
Hastes to his element of tears.
   From hence her various windings rove
To a well ordered stately grove;
This is the palace of the wood,
And court o' th' Royal Oak, where stood   150
The whole nobility, the Pine,
Straight Ash, tall Fir, and wanton Vine;
The proper Cedar, and the rest;
Here she her deeper senses blest;
Admires great Nature in this pile
Floored with green-velvet Camomile,
Garnished with gems of unset fruit,
Supplied still with a self-recruit;
Her bosom wrought with pretty eyes
Of never-planted Strawberries;   160
Where th' wingéd music of the air
Do richly feast and for their fare
Each evening in a silent shade,
Bestow a grateful serenade.
   Thus even tired with delight,
Sated in soul and appetite;
Full of the purple plum and pear,
The golden apple with the fair
Grape, that mirth fain would have taught her,
And nuts which squirrels cracking brought her;   170
She softly lays her weary limbs,
Whilst gentle slumber now begins
To draw the curtains of her eye;
When straight awakened with a cry
And bitter groan, again reposes,
Again a deep sigh interposes.
And now she hears a trembling voice;
Ah can there aught on earth rejoice!

Why wears she this gay livery
Not black as her dark entrails be?   180
Can trees be green, and to the air
Thus prostitute their flowing hair?
Why do they sprout, not withered die?
Must each thing live save wretched I?
Can days triumph in blue and red,
When both their light, and life is fled?
Fly joy on wings of popinjays
To courts of fools, there as your plays
Die, laughed at and forgot; whilst all
That's good mourns at this funeral.   190
Weep all ye Graces, and you sweet
Choir, that at the Hill inspired meet:
Love put thy tapers out that we
And th' world may seem as blind as thee:
And be, since she is lost (ah wound!)
Not Heaven itself by any found.

   Now as a prisoner new cast,
Who sleeps in chains that night his last,
Next morn is waked with a reprieve,
And from his trance not dream bid live;   200
Wonders (his sense not having scope)
Who speaks, his friend, or his false hope.

   So Aramantha heard, but fear
Dares not yet trust her tempting ear:
And as again her arms o' th' ground
Spread pillows for her head, a sound
More dismal makes a swift divorce,
And starts her thus – Rage, Rapine, Force!
Ye blue-flamed daughters o' th' abyss,
Bring all your snakes, here let them hiss;   210
Let not a leaf its freshness keep;
Blast all their roots, and as you creep
And leave behind your deadly slime,
Poison the budding branch in's prime:

Waste the proud bowers of this grove,
That fiends may dwell in it, and move
As in their proper hell, whilst she
Above, laments this tragedy;
Yet pities not our fate; Oh fair
Vow-breaker, now betrothed to th' air;   220
Why by those laws did we not die,
As live but one, Lucasta! why –
As he Lucasta named, a groan
Strangles the fainting passing tone;
But as she heard Lucasta smiles,
Posses her round, she's slipped meanwhiles
Behind the blind of a thick bush,
When each word temp'ring with a blush,
She gently thus bespake: Sad swain,
If mates in woe do ease our pain,   230
Here's one full of that antic grief,
Which stifled would for ever live,
But told expires; pray then reveal
(To show our wound is half to heal)
What mortal nymph or deity
Bewail you thus? Whoe'er you be
The shepherd sighed, my woes I crave
Smothered in me, I in my grave;
Yet be in show or truth a saint,
Or fiend breathe anthems, hear my plaint   240
For her and her breath's symphony,
Which now makes full the harmony
Above, and to whose voice the spheres
Listen, and call her music theirs;
This was I blest on earth with, so
As druids amorous did grow
Jealous of both, for as one day
This star as yet but set in clay
By an embracing river lay,
They steeped her in the hollowed brook   250

Which from her human nature took,
And straight to heaven with wingéd fear,
Thus ravished with her, ravish her.
   The nymph replied, this holy rape
Became the gods, whose obscure shape
They clothed with light, whilst ill you grieve
Your better life should ever live,
And weep that she to whom you wish
What Heaven could give, has all its bliss;
Calling her Angel here, yet be   260
Sad at this true divinity:
She's for the altar not the skies,
Whom first you crown, then sacrifice.
   Fond man thus to a precipice
Aspires, till at the top his eyes
Have lost the safety of the plain,
Then begs of Fate the vales again.
   The now confounded shepherd cries
Ye all confounding Destinies!
How did you make that voice so sweet   270
Without that glorious form to it?
Thou sacred spirit of my Dear
Where'er thou hover'st o'er us hear!
Imbark thee in the laurel tree,
And a new Phoebus follows thee,
Who 'stead of all his burning rays
Will strive to catch thee with his lays;
Or if within the orient vine,
Thou art both deity and wine;
But if thou tak'st the myrtle grove   280
That Paphos is, thou Queen of Love
And I thy swain who (else) must die
By no beast's, but thy cruelty:
But you are rougher than the wind;
Are souls on Earth than Heav'n more kind?
Imprisoned in Mortality,

Lucasta would have answered me.
Lucasta! Aramantha said,
Is she that Virgin-star a maid
Except her prouder livery, 290
In beauty poor, and cheap as I?
Whose glory like a meteor shone,
Or aery Apparition
Admired a while but slighted known.

   Fierce, as the chaféd lion hies,
He rouses him, and to her flies,
Thinking to answer with his spear –
   Now as in war intestine, where
I' th' mist of a black battle, each
Lays at his next, then makes a breach 300
Through th' entrails of another whom
He sees nor knows when he did come
Guided alone by rage and th' drum,
But stripping and impatient wild,
He finds too soon his only child.

   So our expiring desp'rate lover
Fared, when amazed he did discover
Lucasta in this nymph, his sin
Darts the accurséd javelin
'Gainst his own breast, which she puts by 310
With a soft lip and gentle eye,
Then closes with him on the ground
And now her smiles have healed his wound,
Alexis too again is found:
But not until those heavy crimes
She hath kissed off a thousand times,
Who not contented with this pain
Doth threaten to offend again.

   And now they gaze, and sigh, and weep,
Whilst each cheek doth the other's steep, 320
Whilst tongues as exorcised are calm;
Only the rhet'ric of the palm

Prevailing pleads, until at last
They chained in one another fast:
LUCASTA to him doth relate
Her various chance and diff'ring Fate:
How chased by HYDRAPHIL, and tracked,
The num'rous foe to PHILANACT,
Who whilst they for the same things fight,
As BARDS' decrees, and DRUIDS' rite,   330
For safeguard of their proper joys,
And shepherd's freedom, each destroys
The glory of this Sicily;
Since seeking thus the remedy,
They fancy (building on false ground)
The means must them and it confound,
Yet are resolved to stand or fall,
And win a little or lose all.

 From this sad storm of fire and blood
She fled to this yet living wood;   340
Where she 'mongst savage beasts doth find
Herself more safe than human kind.

 Then she relates how CELIA
The Lady here strips her array,
And girdles her in homespun bays,
Then makes her conversant in lays
Of birds, and swains more innocent
That ken not guile or courtshipment.

 Now walks she to her bow'r to dine
Under a shade of Eglantine,   350
Upon a dish of Nature's cheer
Which both grew dressed, and served up there:
That done, she feasts her smell with posies
Plucked from the damask cloth of Roses,
Which there continually doth stay,
And only frost can take away;
Then wagers which hath most content,
Her eye, ear, hand, her gust or scent.

Entranced ALEXIS sees and hears,
As walking above all the spheres: 360
Knows and adores this, and is wild
Until with her he live thus mild.
So that which to his thoughts he meant
For loss of her a punishment,
His arms hung up and his sword broke,
His ensigns folded, he betook
Himself unto the humble Crook:
And for a full reward of all,
She now doth him her shepherd call,
And in a SEE of flow'rs install: 370
Then gives her faith immediately,
Which he returns religiously;
Both vowing in her peaceful cave
To make their bridal-bed and grave.

But the true joy this pair conceived
Each from the other first bereaved;
And then found after such alarms
Fast pinioned in each other's arms:
Ye panting Virgins that do meet
Your loves within their winding-sheet, 380
Breathing and constant still ev'n there;
Or souls their bodies in yon sphere,
Or angels men returned from Hell,
And separated minds can tell.

To Lucasta: Her Reserved Looks

Lucasta frown and let me die,
But smile and see I live;
The sad indifference of your eye
Both kills, and doth reprieve.

You hide our fate within its screen,
   We feel our judgement ere we hear:
So in one picture I have seen
   An angel here, the devil there.

Lucasta Laughing

Hark how she laughs aloud,
Although the world put on its shroud;
Wept at by the fantastic crowd,
   Who cry, One drop let fall
From her, might save the Universal Ball.
     She laughs again
      At our ridiculous pain;
And at our merry misery
    She laughs until she cry;
       Sages, forbear   10
     That ill-contrivéd tear,
      Although your fear,
Doth barricado Hope from your soft ear.
That which still makes her mirth to flow,
   Is our sinister-handed woe,
Which downwards on its head doth go;
   And ere that it is sown, doth grow.
      This makes her spleen contract,
       And her just pleasure feast;
     For the unjustest act   20
      Is still the pleasant'st jest.

Song

Strive not, vain lover, to be fine,
  Thy silk's the silk-worm's, and not thine;
You lessen to a fly your mistress' thought,
To think it may be in a cobweb caught.
  What though her thin transparent lawn
  Thy heart in a strong net hath drawn?
Not all the arms the god of fire e'er made,
Can the soft bulwarks of nak'd love invade.

  Be truly fine then, and yourself dress
  In her fair soul's immac'late glass:
Then by reflection you may have the bliss
Perhaps to see what a true fineness is;
  When all your gauderies will fit
  Those only that are poor in wit:
She that a clinquant outside doth adore,
Dotes on a gilded statue, and no more.

Her Muff

'Twas not for some calm blessing to deceive,
Thou didst thy polish'd hands in shagg'd furs weave;
  It were no blessing thus obtained,
  Thou rather wouldst a curse have gained,
Than let thy warm driven snow be ever stained.

Not that you fearéd the discol'ring cold,
Might alchemise their silver into gold;
  Nor could your ten white nuns so sin,
  That you should thus penance them in
Each in her coarse hair smock of discipline.   10

Nor Hero-like, who on their crest still wore
A lion, panther, leopard or a boar,
  To look their enemies in their hearse;
  Thou wouldst thy hand should deeper pierce,
And, in its softness rough, appear more fierce.

No, no, Lucasta, destiny decreed
That beasts to thee a sacrifice should bleed,
  And strip themselves to make you gay;
  For ne'er yet herald did display,
A coat, where sables upon ermine lay.   20

This for lay-lovers, that must stand at door,
Salute the threshold, and admire no more:
  But I, in my invention tough,
  Rate not this outward bliss enough,
But still contemplate must the hidden muff.

Lucasta at the Bath

I' th' autumn of a summer's day,
When all the winds got leave to play;
Lucasta, that fair ship, is launched,
And from its crust this almond blanched.

Blow then, unruly North-wind, blow,
Till in their holds your eyes you stow;
And swell your cheeks, bequeath chill Death:
See! she hath smiled thee out of breath.

Court gentle Zephyr, court and fan
Her softer breast's carnationed wan;   10
Your charming rhetoric of down
Flies scattered from before her frown.

Say, my white water-lily, say,
How is't those warm streams break away?
Cut by thy chaste cold breast which dwells
Amidst them armed in icicles.

And the hot floods more raging grown
In flames of thee, than in their own;
In their distempers wildly glow,
And kiss thy pillar of fixed snow.   20

No sulphur, through whose each blue vein
The thick and lazy currents strain,
Can cure the smarting, nor the fell
Blisters of love wherewith they swell.

These great physicians of the blind,
The lame, and fatal blains of Inde,
In every drop themselves now see
Speckled with a new leprosy.

As sick drinks are with old wine dashed,
Foul waters too with spirits washed;   30
Thou grieved, perchance, one tear let'st fall,
Which straight did purify them all.

And now is cleansed enough the flood,
Which since runs clear, as doth thy blood;
Of the wet pearls uncrown thy hair,
And mantle thee with ermine air.

Lucasta, hail! fair conqueress
Of fire, air, earth, and seas;
Thou whom all kneel to, yet even thou
Wilt unto Love, thy captive, bow.

The Ant

Forbear thou great good husband, little ant;
  A little respite from thy flood of sweat;
Thou, thine own horse and cart, under this plant
  Thy spacious tent, fan thy prodigious heat;
Down with thy double load of that one grain;
It is a granary for all thy train.

Cease large example of wise thrift a while,
  (For thy example is become our law)
And teach thy frowns a seasonable smile:
  So Cato sometimes the nak'd Florals saw.   10
And thou almighty foe, lay by thy sting,
Whilst thy unpaid musicians, crickets, sing.

Lucasta, she that holy makes the day,
  And 'stills new life in fields of fueillemort:
Hath back restored their verdure with one ray,
  And with her eye bid all to play and sport.
Ant to work still; Age will thee truant call;
And to save now, th' art worse than prodigal.

Austere and Cynic! not one hour t' allow,
  To lose with pleasure what thou gotst with pain: 20
But drive on sacred festivals, thy plough;
  Tearing highways with thy o'er chargéd wain.
Not all thy lifetime one poor minute live,
And thy o'er laboured bulk with mirth relieve?

Look up then miserable ant, and spy
  Thy fatal foes, for breaking of her law,
Hov'ring above thee, Madam Margaret Pie,
  And her fierce servant, meagre Sir John Daw:
Thy self and storehouse now they do store up,
And thy whole harvest too within their crop. 30

Thus we unthrifty thrive within Earth's tomb,
   For some more rav'nous and ambitious jaw:
The grain in th' ant's, the ant's in the pie's womb,
   The pie in th' hawk's, the hawk's i' th' eagle's maw:
So scattering to hoard 'gainst a long day,
Thinking to save all, we cast all away.

The Snail

Wise emblem of our politic world,
Sage snail, within thine own self curled;
Instruct me softly to make haste,
Whilst these my feet go slowly fast.
   Compendious snail! thou seem'st to me,
Large Euclid's strict epitome;
And in each diagram, dost fling
Thee from the point unto the ring.
A figure now triangular,
An oval now, and now a square;   10
And then a serpentine dost crawl
Now a straight line, now crook'd, now all.
   Preventing rival of the day,
Th' art up and openest thy ray,
And ere the morn cradles the moon,
Th' art broke into a beauteous noon.
Then when the sun sups in the deep,
Thy silver horns ere Cynthia's peep;
And thou from thine own liquid bed
New Phoebus heav'st thy pleasant head.   20
   Who shall a name for thee create,
Deep riddle of mysterious state?
Bold Nature that gives common birth
To all products of seas and Earth,

Of thee, as earthquakes, is afraid,
Nor will thy dire deliv'ry aid.
  Thou thine own daughter then, and sire,
That son and mother art entire,
That big still with thyself dost go,
And liv'st an aged embryo;   30
That like the cubs of India,
Thou from thyself a while dost play:
But frighted with a dog or gun,
In thine own belly thou dost run,
And as thy house was thine own womb,
So thine own womb, concludes thy tomb.
  But now I must (analysed king)
Thy economic virtues sing;
Thou great staid husband still within,
Thou, thee, that's thine dost discipline;   40
And when thou art to progress bent,
Thou mov'st thyself and tenement,
As warlike Scythians travelled, you
Remove your men and city too;
Then after a sad dearth and rain,
Thou scatterest thy silver train;
And when the trees grow nak'd and old,
Thou clothést them with cloth of gold,
Which from thy bowels thou dost spin,
And draw from the rich mines within.   50
  Now hast thou chang'd thee saint; and made
Thyself a fane that cupola'd;
And in thy wreathéd cloister thou
Walkest thine own grey friar too;
Strict, and locked up, th' art hood all o'er
And ne'er eliminat'st thy door.
On salads thou dost feed severe,
And 'stead of beads thou drop'st a tear,
And when to rest, each calls the bell,
Thou sleep'st within thy marble cell;   60

Where in dark contemplation placed,
The sweets of Nature thou dost taste;
Who now with Time thy days resolve,
And in a jelly thee dissolve.
Like a shot star, which doth repair
Upward, and rarify the air.

A Loose Saraband

Nay, prithee dear, draw nigher,
  Yet closer nigher yet;
Here is a double fire,
  A dry one and a wet:
True lasting heavenly fuel
Puts out the vestal jewel,
When once we twining marry
Mad Love with wild Canary.

Off with that crownéd Venice
  Till all the house doth flame,   10
We'll quench it straight in Rhenish,
  Or what we must not name:
Milk lightning still assuageth,
So when our fury rageth,
As th' only means to cross it,
We'll drown it in Love's posset.

Love never was well-willer,
  Unto my nag or me,
Ne'er watered us i' th' cellar,
  But the cheap buttery: 20
At th' head of his own barrels,
Where broached are all his quarrels,

Should a true noble master
Still make his guest his taster.

See all the world how't staggers,
   More ugly drunk than we,
As if far gone in daggers,
   And blood it seemed to be:
We drink our glass of roses,
Which nought but sweets discloses,   30
Then in our loyal chamber,
Refresh us with Love's amber.

Now tell me, thou fair cripple,
   That dumb canst scarcely see
Th' almightiness of tipple,
   And th' odds 'twixt thee and thee:
What of Elysium's missing?
Still drinking and still kissing;
Adoring plump October;
Lord! what is man and sober?   40

Now, is there such a trifle
   As Honour, the fool's giant?
What is there left to rifle,
   When wine makes all parts pliant?
Let others glory follow,
In their false riches wallow,
And with their grief be merry;
Leave me but love and sherry.

The Falcon

Fair Princess of the spacious air,
That hast vouchsafed acquaintance here,
With us are quartered below stairs,
That can reach Heaven with nought but prayers;
Who when our activ'st wings we try,
Advance a foot into the sky.

Bright heir t' th' Bird Imperial,
From whose avenging pennons fall
Thunder and lightning twisted spun;
Brave cousin-german to the sun,   10
That didst forsake thy throne and sphere,
To be an humble pris'ner here;
And for a perch of her soft hand,
Resign the Royal Wood's command.

How often wouldst thou shoot Heaven's arc,
Then mount thyself into a lark;
And after our short faint eyes call,
When now a fly, now nought at all;
Then stoop so swift unto our sense,
As thou wert sent intelligence.   20

Free beauteous slave, thy happy feet
In silver fetters varvels meet,
And trample on that noble wrist
The gods have kneeled in vain t' have kissed:
But gaze not, bold deceivéd spy,
Too much o' th' lustre of her eye;
The sun, thou dost out-stare, alas!
Winks at the glory of her face.

Be safe then in thy velvet helm,
Her looks are calms that do o'erwhelm,   30

Than the Arabian bird more blest,
Chafe in the spicery of her breast,
And lose you in her breath, a wind
Sours the delicious gales of Inde.

But now a quill from thine own wing
I pluck, thy lofty fate to sing;
Whilst we behold the various fight,
With mingled pleasure and affright,
The humbler hinds do fall to prayer,
As when an army's seen i' th' air   40
And the prophetic spaniels run,
And howl thy epicedium.

The Heron mounted doth appear
On his own Peg'sus a lanceer,
And seems on earth, when he doth hut,
A proper halberdier on foot;
Secure i' th' moor, about to sup,
The dogs have beat his quarters up.

And now he takes the open air,
Draws up his wings with tactic care;   50
Whilst th' expert falcon swift doth climb,
In subtle mazes serpentine;
And to advantage closely twined
She gets the upper sky and wind,
Where she dissembles to invade,
And lies a pol'tic ambuscade.

The hedged-in heron, whom the foe
Awaits above, and dogs below,
In his fortification lies,
And makes him ready for surprise;   60
When rouséd with a shrill alarm,
Was shouted from beneath, they arm.

73

The falcon charges at first view
With her brigade of talons; through
Whose shoots, the wary heron beat,
With a well counterwheeled retreat.
But the bold gen'ral never lost,
Hath won again her airy post;
Who wild in this affront, now fries,
Then gives a volley of her eyes.   70

    The desp'rate heron now contracts,
In one design all former facts;
Noble he is resolv'd to fall
His, and his en'my's funeral,
And (to be rid of her) to die
A public martyr of the sky.

    When now he turns his last to wreak
The palisadoes of his beak;
The raging foe impatient
Wrack'd with revenge, and fury rent,   80
Swift as the thunderbolt he strikes,
Too sure upon the stand of pikes,
There she his naked breast doth hit
And on the case of rapiers 's split.

    But ev'n in her expiring pangs
The heron's pounced within her fangs,
And so above she stoops to rise
A trophy and a sacrifice;
Whilst her own bells in the sad fall
Ring out the double funeral.   90

    Ah victory! unhap'ly won,
Weeping and red is set the sun,
Whilst the whole field floats in one tear,
And all the air doth mourning wear:

74

Close hooded all thy kindred come
To pay their vows upon thy tomb;
The hobby and the musket too,
Do march to take their last adieu.

The lanner and the lanneret,
The colours bear as banneret;   100
The goshawk and her tercel roused,
With tears attend thee as new boused,
All these are in their dark array
Led by the various herald-jay.

But thy eternal name shall live
Whilst quills from ashes fame reprieve,
Whilst open stands renown's wide door,
And wings are left on which to soar;
Doctor Robin, the prelate Pie,
And the poetic Swan shall die,   110
Only to sing thy elegy.

Love Made in the First Age: To Chloris

In the nativity of time,
Chloris! it was not thought a crime
    In direct Hebrew for to woo.
Now we make love, as all on fire,
Ring retrograde our loud desire,
    And court in English backward too.

Thrice happy was that golden age,
When compliment was construed rage,
    And fine words in the centre hid;
When cursed No stained no maid's bliss,   10

And all discourse was summed in Yes,
   And nought forbad, but to forbid.

Love then unstinted, Love did sip,
And cherries plucked fresh from the lip,
   On cheeks and roses free he fed;
Lasses like autumn plums did drop,
And lads, indifferently did crop
   A flower, and a maidenhead.

Then unconfinéd each did tipple
Wine from the bunch, milk from the nipple,   20
   Paps tractable as udders were;
Then equally the wholesome jellies,
Were squeezed from olive-trees, and bellies,
   Nor suits of trespass did they fear.

A fragrant bank of strawberries,
Diapered with violets' eyes,
   Was table, table-cloth, and fare;
No palace to the clouds did swell,
Each humble princess then did dwell
   In the piazza of her hair.   30

Both broken faith, and th' cause of it,
All damning gold was damned to th' pit;
   Their troth sealed with a clasp and kiss,
Lasted until that extreme day,
In which they smiled their souls away,
   And in each other breathed new bliss.

Because no fault, there was no tear;
No groan did grate the granting ear;
   No false foul breath their del'cate smell:
No serpent kiss poisoned the taste,   40
Each touch was naturally chaste,
   And their mere sense a miracle.

Naked as their own innocence,
And unembroidered from offence
  They went, above poor riches, gay;
On softer than the cygnet's down,
In beds they tumbled of their own;
  For each within the other lay.

Thus did they live: Thus did they love,
Repeating only joys above;   50
  And angels were, but with clothes on,
Which they would put off cheerfully,
To bathe them in the galaxy,
  Then gird them with the heavenly zone.

Now, Chloris! miserably crave,
The offered bliss you would not have;
  Which evermore I must deny,
Whilst ravished with these noble dreams,
And crownéd with mine own soft beams,
  Enjoying of myself I lie.   60

To a Lady with child that asked an Old Shirt

And why an honoured ragged shirt, that shows,
Like tattered ensigns, all its body's blows?
Should it be swathéd in a vest so dire,
It were enough to set the child on fire;
Dishevelled queens should strip them of their hair,
And in it mantle the new rising heir:
Nor do I know aught worth to wrap it in,
Except my parchment upper-coat of skin:
And then expect no end of its chaste tears,
That first was rolled in down, now furs of bears.   10

But since to ladies 't hath a custom been
Linen to send, that travail and lie in;
To the nine sempstresses, my former friends,
I sued, but they had nought but shreds and ends.
At last, the jolli'st of the three times three,
Rent th' apron from her smock, and gave it me,
'Twas soft and gentle, subtly spun no doubt;
Pardon my boldness, Madam; *Here's the clout*.

Cupid Far Gone

What so beyond all madness is the elf,
  Now he hath got out of himself!
  His fatal enemy the bee,
  Nor his deceived artillery;
  His shackles, nor the rose's bough
Ne'er half so nettled him as he is now.

See! at's own mother he is offering,
  His finger now fits any ring;
  Old Cybele he would enjoy,
  And now the girl, and now the boy.   10
  He proffers Jove a back caress,
And all his love in the antipodes.

Jealous of his chaste Psyche, raging he,
  Quarrels the student Mercury;
  And with a proud submissive breath
  Offers to change his darts with Death.
  He strikes at the bright Eye of Day,
And Juno tumbles in her milky way.

The dear sweet secrets of the gods he tells,
    And with loathed hate loved heaven he swells;   20
    Now like a fury he belies
    Myriads of pure virginities;
    And swears, with this false frenzy hurled,
There's not a virtuous she in all the world.

Olympus he renounces, then descends,
    And makes a friendship with the fiends;
    Bids Charon be no more a slave,
    He Argus rigged with stars shall have;
    And triple Cerberus from below
Must leashed t' himself with him a hunting go.   30

A Mock-Song

    Now Whitehall's in the grave,
    And our Head is our slave,
The bright pearl in his close shell of oyster;
    Now the Mitre is lost,
    The proud Prelates, too, crossed,
And all Rome's confined to a cloister:
    He that Tarquin was styled,
    Our white Land's exiled,
    Yea undefiled,
Not a Court Ape's left to confute us: 10
    Then let your voices rise high,
    As your colours did fly,
    And flour'shing cry,
Long live the brave Oliver-Brutus.

Now the Sun is unarmed,
And the Moon by us charmed,
All the Stars dissolved to a jelly;
Now the Thighs of the Crown,
And the Arms are lopped down,
And the Body is all but a belly: 20
Let the Commons go on,
The Town is our own,
We'll rule alone;
For the Knights have yielded their Spent-gorge;
And an order is ta'en,
With HONY SOIT profane,
Shout forth amain,
For our Dragon hath vanquished the St. George.

A Fly Caught in a Cobweb

Small type of great ones, that do hum,
Within this whole world's narrow room,
That with a busy hollow noise
Catch at the people's vainer voice,
And with spread sails play with their breath,
Whose very hails new christen Death.
Poor fly caught in an airy net,
Thy wings have fettered now thy feet;
Where like a lion in a toil,
Howe'er, thou keep'st a noble coil,   10
And beat'st thy gen'rous breast, that o'er
The plains thy fatal buzzes roar,
Till thy all-bellied foe (round elf)
Hath quartered thee within himself.
Was it not better once to play
I' th' light of a majestic ray?

Where though too near and bold, the fire
Might singe thy upper down attire,
And thou i' th' storm to lose an eye,
A wing, or a self-trapping thigh;　　　　　　　　　　20
Yet hadst thou fall'n like him, whose coil
Made fishes in the sea to broil;
When now th'ast scaped the noble flame,
Trapped basely in a slimy frame;
And free of air, thou art become
Slave to the spawn of mud and loam.
　　Nor is't enough thyself dost dress
To thy swoll'n lord a num'rous mess,
And by degrees thy thin veins bleed,
And piece-meal dost his poison feed;　　　　　　　30
But now devoured, art like to be
A net spun for thy family
And straight expanded in the air
Hang'st for thy issue too a snare.
Strange witty death, and cruel ill,
That killing thee, thou thine dost kill!
Like pies in whose entombéd ark,
All fowl crowd downward to a lark;
Thou art thine en'my's sepulchre,
And in thee buriest too thine heir.　　　　　　　　40
　　Yet Fates a glory have reserved
For one so highly hath deserved;
As the rhinocerous doth die
Under his castle-enemy,
As through the crane's trunk throat doth speed,
The asp doth on his feeder feed;
Fall yet triumphant in thy woe,
Bound with the entrails of thy foe.

A Fly About a Glass of Burnt Claret

Forbear this liquid fire, Fly,
It is more fatal than the dry,
That singly, but embracing, wounds,
And this at once, both burns and drowns.

The salamander that in heat
And flames doth cool his monstrous sweat;
Whose fan a glowing cake, 'tis said,
Of this red furnace is afraid.

Viewing the ruby-crystal shine,
Thou tak'st it for heaven-crystalline;   10
Anon thou wilt be taught to groan,
'Tis an ascended Acheron.

A snowball-heart in it let fall,
And take it out a fire-ball:
An icy breast in it betrayed,
Breaks a destructive wild grenade.

'Tis this makes Venus' altars shine,
This kindles frosty Hymen's pine;
When the boy grows old in his desires,
This flambeau doth new light his fires.   20

Though the cold hermit ever wail,
Whose sighs do freeze, and tears drop hail,
Once having passéd this, will ne'er
Another flaming purging fear.

The Vestal drinking this doth burn,
Now more than in her fun'ral urn;
Her fires, that with the sun kept race,
Are now extinguish'd by her face.

The chemist, that himself doth 'still,
Let him but taste this limbeck's bill,   30
And prove this sublimated bowl,
He'll swear it will calcine a soul.

Noble and brave! now thou dost know,
The false preparéd decks below,
Dost thou the fatal liquor sup,
One drop alas! thy bark blows up.

What airy country hast to save,
Whose plagues thou'lt bury in thy grave?
For even now thou seem'st to us
On this gulf's brink a Curtius.   40

And now th' art fall'n (magnanimous fly)
In, where thine ocean doth fry,
Like the sun's son who blushed the flood,
To a complexion of blood.

Yet see! my glad auricular
Redeems thee (though dissolved) a star,
Flaggy thy wings, and scorched thy thighs,
Thou li'st a double sacrifice.

And now my warming, cooling breath
Shall a new life afford in death;   50
See! in the hospital of my hand
Already cured, thou fierce dost stand.

Burnt insect! dost thou reaspire
The moist-hot-glass, and liquid fire?
I see! 'tis such a pleasing pain,
Thou wouldst be scorched, and drowned again.

Advice to my Best Brother. Colonel Francis Lovelace.

Frank, wilt live handsomely? trust not too far
Thyself to waving seas, for what thy star
Calculated by sure event must be,
Look in the glassy-epithet and see.

Yet settle here your rest, and take your state,
And in calm halcyon's nest ev'n build your fate;
Prithee lie down securely, Frank, and keep
With as much no noise the inconstant deep
As its inhabitants; nay steadfast stand
As if discovered were a New-found-land   10
Fit for plantation here; dream, dream still,
Lulled in Dione's cradle, dream, until
Horror awake your sense, and you now find
Yourself a bubbled pastime for the wind,
And in loose Thetis' blankets torn and tossed;
Frank to undo thyself why art at cost?

Nor be too confident, fixed on the shore,
For even that too borrows from the store
Of her rich neighbour, since now wisest know,
(And this to Galileo's judgment owe)   20
The palsy Earth itself is every jot
As frail, inconstant, waving as that blot
We lay upon the deep, that sometimes lies
Changed, you would think, with's bottom's properties;
But this eternal strange Ixion's wheel
Of giddy earth, ne'er whirling leaves to reel
Till all things are inverted, till they are
Turned to that antic confused state they were.

Who loves the golden mean, doth safely want
A cobwebbed cot, and wrongs entailed upon't;   30
He richly needs a palace for to breed

84

Vipers and moths, that on their feeder feed.
The toy that we (too true) a mistress call,
Whose looking-glass and feather weighs up all;
And clothes which larks would play with, in the sun,
That mock him in the night when's course is run.

    To rear an edifice by art so high
That envy should not reach it with her eye,
Nay with a thought come near it, wouldst thou know
How such a structure should be raised? build low.   40
The blust'ring wind's invisible rough stroke,
More often shakes the stubborn'st, prop'rest oak,
And in proud turrets we behold withal,
'Tis the imperial top declines to fall.
Nor does Heaven's lightning strike the humble vales
But high aspiring mounts batters and scales.

    A breast of proof defies all shocks of fate,
Fears in the best, hopes in the worser state;
Heaven forbid that, as of old, Time ever
Flourished in Spring, so contrary, now never: 50
That mighty breath which blew foul Winter hither,
Can eas'ly puff it to a fairer weather.
Why dost despair then, Frank? Aelos has
A Zephyrus as well as Boreas.

    'Tis a false sequel, solecism, 'gainst those
Precepts giv'n us, to suppose
That 'cause it is now ill, 't will e'er be so;
Apollo doth not always bend his bow;
But oft uncrownéd of his beams divine,
With his soft harps awakes the sleeping Nine.   60

    In strictest things magnanimous appear,
Greater in hope, howe'er thy fate, than fear:
Draw all your sails in quickly, though no storm

Threaten your ruin with a sad alarm;
For tell me how they differ, tell me pray,
A cloudy tempest, and a too fair day.

To Dr. F.B. On his Book of Chess

Sir, now unravelled is the Golden Fleece:
Men that could only fool at Fox and Geese,
Are new made politicians by thy book,
And both can judge and conquer with a look.
The hidden fate of princes you unfold;
Court, clergy, Commons, by your law controlled;
   Strange, serious wantoning, all that they
    Blustered, and cluttered for, *you play*.

On Sannazar's being honoured with six hundred ducats by the Clarissimi of Venice, for composing an Elegiac Hexastich of the City. A Satire.

'Twas a blithe prince exchanged five hundred crowns
For a fair turnip; dig, dig on, O clowns!
But how this comes about, Fates can you tell,
This more than Maid of Meurs, this miracle?
Let me not live, if I think not St. Mark
Has all the oar, as well as beasts in's ark;
No wonder 'tis he marries the rich sea,
But to betroth him to nak'd Poesie,
And with a bankrupt Muse to merchandise,
His treasure's beams sure have put out his eyes.   10
His conquest at Lepanto I'll let pass,

When the sick sea with turbans night-capped was;
And now at Candie his full courage shown,
That waned to a wan line the half-half moon;
This is a wreath, this is a victory,
Caesar himself would have looked pale to see,
And in the height of all his triumphs, feel
Himself but chained to such a mighty wheel.
   And now methinks we ape Augustus' state,
So ugly we his high worth imitate,   20
Monkey his godlike glories; so that we
Keep light and form, with such deformity,
As I have seen an arrogant baboon
With a small piece of glass zany the sun.
   Rome to her bard, who did her battles sing,
Indifferent gave to poet and to king;
With the same laurels were his temples fraught
Who best had written, and who best had fought;
The selfsame fame they equally did feel,
One's style adored as much as th' other's steel.   30
A chain or fasces she could then afford
The sons of Phoebus, we an axe, or cord;
Sometimes a coronet was her renown,
And ours the dear prerogative of a crown.
In marble statued walks great Lucan lay,
And now we walk our own pale statua:
They the whole year with roses crowned would dine,
And we in all December know no wine;
Disciplined, dieted, sure there hath been,
Odds 'twixt a poet and a capuchin.   40
   Of princes, women, wine, to sing I see
Is no Apocrypha; for to rise high
Commend this Olio of this lord, 'tis fit,
Nay ten to one but you have part of it;
There is that justice left, since you maintain
His table, he should counter-feed your brain.
Then write how well he in his sack hath drolled,

Straight there's a bottle to your chamber rolled.
Or with embroidered words praise his French suit,
Month hence 'tis yours, with his man's curse to boot;   50
Or but applaud his bossed legs, two to none,
But he most nobly doth give you one:
Or spin an elegy on his false hair,
'Tis well he cries, but living hair is dear;
Yet say that out of order there's one curl,
And all the hopes of your reward you furl.
    Write a deep epic poem, and you may
As soon delight them as the Opera,
Where they Diogenes thought in his tub,
Never so sour did look, so sweet a club.   60
    You that do suck for thirst your black quill's blood,
And chew your laboured papers for your food,
I will inform you how and what to praise,
Then skin y' in satin as young Lovelace plays.
Beware, as you would your fierce guests, your lice,
To strip the cloth of gold from cherished vice;
Rather stand off with awe and reverend fear,
Hang a poetic pendant in her ear.
Court her as her adorers do their glass,
Though that as much of a true substance has,   70
Whilst all the gall from your wild ink you drain,
The beauteous sweets of virtue's cheeks to stain;
And in your livery let her be known,
As poor and tatteréd as in her own.
Nor write, nor speak you more of sacred writ,
But what shall force up your arrested wit.
Be chaste religion, and her priests your scorn,
Whilst the vain fanes of idiots you adorn.
It is a mortal error you must know,
Of any to speak good, if he be so.   80
Rail till your edged breath flay your raw throat,
And burn all marks on all of gen'rous note;
Each verse be an indictment, be not free

Sanctity 'tself from thy scurrility.
Libel your father, and your dam buffoon,
The noblest matrons of the isle lampoon,
Whilst Aretine and 's bodies you dispute,
And in your sheets your sister prostitute.
   Yet there belongs a sweetness, softness too,
Which you must pay, but first pray know to who.   90
There is a creature, (if I may so call
That unto which they do all prostrate fall)
Termed Mistress, when they're angry, but pleased high,
It is a Princess, Saint, Divinity.
To this they sacrifice the whole day's light,
Then lie with their devotion all night;
For this you are to dive to the abyss,
And rob for pearl the closet of some fish.
Arabia and Sabaea you must strip
Of all their sweets, for to supply her lip;   100
And steal new fire from heav'n for to repair
Her unfledged scalp with Berenice's hair;
Then seat her in Cassiopeia's chair,
As now you're in your coach. Save you bright sir
(O spare your thanks) is not this finer far
Than walk un-hided, when that every stone
Has knocked acquaintance with your ankle bone?
When your winged papers, like the last dove, ne'er
Returned to quit you of your hope or fear,
But left you to the mercy of your host,   110
And your day's fare, a fortifiéd toast.
   How many battles sung in epic strain,
Would have procured your head thatch from the rain?
Not all the arms of Thebes and Troy would get
One knife but to anatomize your meat,
A funeral elegy with a sad boon
Might make you (*hei*) sip wine like Macaroon;
But if perchance there did a ribbon come,
Not the train-band so fierce with all its drum,

Yet with your torch you homeward would retire,   120
And heart'ly wish your bed your fun'ral pyre.
   With what a fury have I known you feed,
Upon a contract, and the hopes 't might speed;
Not the fair bride, impatient of delay,
Doth wish like you the beauties of that day;
Hotter than all the roasted cooks you sat
To dress the fricace of your alphabet,
Which sometimes would be drawn dough anagram,
Sometimes acrostic parchéd in the flame;
Then posies stewed with sippets, mottoes by,   130
Of mincéd verse a miserable pie.
How many knots slipped e'er you twist their name,
With th' old device, as both their hearts the same:
Whilst like to drills the feast in your false jaw,
You would transmit at leisure to your maw;
Then after all your fooling, fat, and wine,
Gluttoned at last, return at home to pine.
   Tell me, O Sun, since first your beams did play
To Night, and did awake the sleeping day;
Since first your steeds of light their race did start,   140
Did you e'er blush as now? Oh thou that art
The common Father to the base pismire,
As well as great Alcides, did the fire,
From thine own altar which the gods adore,
Kindle the souls of gnats and wasps before?
   Who would delight in his chaste eyes to see,
Dormice to strike at lights of poesy?
Faction and Envy now is downright rage;
Once a five-knotted whip there was, the Stage,
The beadle and the executioner,   150
To whip small errors, and the great ones tear.
Now as ere Nimrod the first king, he writes,
That's strongest, th' ablest deepest bites.
The Muses weeping fly their hill, to see
Their noblest sons of peace in mutiny.

Could there nought else this civil war complete,
But poets raging with poetic heat,
Tearing themselves and th' endless wreath, as though
Immortal they, their wrath should be so too;
And doubly fired Apollo burns to see   160
In silent Helicon a naumachy.
Parnassus hears these as his first alarms,
Never till now Minerva was in arms.

　　O more than conqu'ror of the world, great Rome!
Thy heroes did with gentleness o'ercome
Thy foes themselves, but one another first,
Whilst Envy stripped, alone was left, and burst.
The learn'd Decemviri, 'tis true did strive,
But to add flames to keep their fame alive;
Whilst the eternal laurel hung i' th' air;   170
Nor of these ten sons was there found one heir,
Like to the golden tripod it did pass,
From this to this, till 't came to him whose 't was:
Caesar to Gallus trundled it, and he
To Maro, Maro, Naso unto thee;
Naso to his Tibullus flung the wreath,
He to Catullus: thus did each bequeath,
This glorious circle to another round,
At last the temples of their god it bound.

　　I might believe, at least, that each might have   180
A quiet fame contented in his grave,
Envy the living, not the dead, doth bite,
For after death all men receive their right.
If it be sacrilege for to profane
Their holy ashes, what is't then their flame?
He does that wrong unweeting or in ire,
As if one should put out the vestal fire.

　　Let Earth's four quarters speak, and thou Sun bear
Now witness for thy fellow-traveller,
I was allied dear *uncle* unto thee   190
In blood, but thou alas not unto me;

Your virtues, pow'rs, and mine differed at best,
As they whose springs you saw, the East and West:
Let me a while be twisted in thy shine,
And pay my due devotions at thy shrine.
  Might learned *Wenman* rise, who went with thee
In thy Heaven's work beside divinity,
I should sit still; or mighty *Falkland* stand,
To justify with breath his pow'rful hand;
The glory that doth circle your pale urn   200
Might hallowed still and undefiléd burn;
But I forbear; flames that are wildly thrown
At sacred heads, curl back upon their own;
Sleep heavenly *Sandys*, whilst what they do or write,
Is to give God himself and you your right.
  There is not in my mind one sullen Fate
Of old, but is concentred in our state.
Vandal o'er-runners, Goths in literature,
Ploughmen that would Parnassus new manure;
  Ringers of verse that all-in all-in chime,   210
And toll the changes upon every rhyme.
A mercer now by th' yard does measure o'er
An ode which was but by the foot before;
Deals you an ell of epigram, and swears
It is the strongest and the finest wares.
No wonder if a drawer verses rack,
If 'tis not his 't may be the spir't of sack;
Whilst the fair bar-maid strokes the Muse's teat,
For milk to make the posset up complete.
  Arise thou rev'rend shade, great Jonson rise!   220
Break through thy marble natural disguise;
Behold a mist of insects, whose mere breath,
Will melt thy hallowed leaden house of death.
What was Crispinus that you should defy
The age for him? He durst not look so high
As your immortal rod, he still did stand
Honoured, and held his forehead to thy brand.

These scorpions with which we have to do,
Are fiends, not only small but deadly too.
Well might'st thou rive thy quill up to the back   230
And screw thy lyre's grave chords until they crack.
For though once Hell resented music, these
Devils will not, but are in worse disease.
How would thy masc'line spirit, Father *Ben*,
Sweat to behold basely deposéd men,
Justled from the prerog'tive of their bed,
Whilst wives are per'wigged with their husband's head.
Each snatches the male quill from his faint hand
And must both nobler write and understand,
He to her fury the soft plume doth bow,   240
O Pen, ne'er truly justly slit till now!
Now as herself a poem she doth dress,
And curls a line as she would do a tress;
Powders a sonnet as she does her hair,
Then prostitutes them both to public air.
Nor is't enough that they their faces blind
With a false dye, but they must paint their mind;
In metre scold, and in scanned order brawl,
Yet there's one *Sappho* left may save them all.
    But now let me recall my passion,   250
Oh (from a noble father, nobler son!)
You that alone are the Clarissimi,
And the whole gen'rous state of Venice be,
It shall not be recorded Sannazar
Shall boast enthroned alone this new made star;
You whose correcting sweetness hath forbade
Shame to the good, and glory to the bad,
Whose honour hath ev'n into virtue tamed,
These swarms that now so angerly I named.
Forgive what thus distempered I indite,   260
For it is hard a satire not to write.
Yet as a virgin that heats all her blood,
At the first motion of bad understood,

93

Then at mere thought of fair chastity,
Straight cools again the tempests of her sea;
  So when to you I my devotions raise,
    All wrath and storms do end in calms and praise.

Notes

p.21 *To Lucasta, Going beyond the Seas* In *Lucasta* the title is prefixed by 'Song. Set by Mr Henry Lawes'. The name *Lucasta*
means 'chaste light'. Various attempts have been made to
identify her, beginning with Anthony Wood's claim that
she was a 'gentlewoman of great beauty and fortune named
Lucy Sachaverel'. Wilkinson guesses that she was probably
a member of the Lucas family, hence the name *Lucasta*.
Beyond the seas was a common seventeenth-century turn
of phrase.

9   *suage* assuage
10 *blue-god* Neptune
13 *betwixt* the emendation to *be 'twixt* has been suggested,
to make better sense of the syntax, but Lovelace is often
elliptical in expression.
15 *separated* one of Lovelace's favourite words: see his use
of it in the last line of *Aramantha* (p.62)

p.22 *To Lucasta, Going to the Wars* The title is prefixed by 'Song.
Set by Mr John Laniere'. For discussion of this poem, see
the essay by G.F. Jones in *Comparative Literature*, 11, 1959,
pp. 131-43; and the debate between N.N. Holland and
R. Rogers in *Literature and Psychology*, 14, 1964, pp. 43-55
& 116-27.
4   *fly* spelt *flie* in the text, it has been suggested that Lovelace meant it to be pronounced *flee*, and this might be a
better modernization.

p.22 *A Paradox*
18 *grot* grotto
19 *heavenly Sidney* i.e. Philip Sidney's *Arcadia*
21 *so new* i.e. so long as it's new
26 *the wisest* Zeus

p.23 *To Aramantha, That she would dishevel her hair* The title is
prefixed by 'Song. Set by Mr Henry Lawes'.

11   *clue*   ball of thread

p.24 *Gratiana dancing and singing*
5   *winding*   melodic variation
7   *pavement*   paved floor

p.25 *The Scrutiny*   The title is followed by 'Song. Set by Mr Thomas Charles'. Behind the title lies the etymology of the word *scrutiny*, from the Latin *scrutari*, 'to search among the trash and rags'.
5   *fond*   foolish
14   *min'ralists*   mineralogists

p.26 *A Loose Saraband*   The title is followed by 'Set by Mr Henry Lawes'. A *saraband* is a 'slow and stately Spanish dance in triple time' (OED), but *loose* means 'wanton', making it a licentious parody of the old dance.
5   *purchase*   acquisition, capture
19   *morning-cushionet*   pin-cushion
20   *'s mother*   Venus, the mother of Cupid
31   *sleeve-silk*   fine silk thread, for use in embroidery
37   *nard*   aromatic ointment

p.28 *The Grasshopper*   The Charles Cotton referred to in this title is the father of the poet of the same name, who died in 1658. For discussions of the poem, see D.C. Allen's essay in *Modern Language Quarterly*, 18, 1957, pp. 35-43 (reprinted in Allen's *Image and Meaning: Metaphoric Traditions in Renaissance Poetry*, pp. 80-92); and Bruce King's essay in *College English*, 26, 1965, pp. 511-15.
10   *gilt-plaits*   golden patches
19   *poise*   counterbalance: cp. Lovelace's use of the noun in *Gratiana dancing and singing*, line 5.
26   *vestal flames*   the sacred flame in the Temple of Vesta at Rome
30   *th' usurping of his reign*   Parliament had banned the celebration of Christmas since 1644.

31   *old Greek*   Greek poems: *The Grasshopper* itself is based on one of the *Anacreonata* (no. 34: see Allen's essay).
32   *he hath his crown again*   perhaps 'king' Christmas, or Charles I (or both)
33   *Hesper*   the evening star

p.29 *The Vintage to the Dungeon*   The title is followed by 'A Song. Set by Mr William Lawes'.
7   *manacle the mind*   an interesting anticipation of Blake's 'mind forged manacles'.

p.30 *To Lucasta. From Prison*   The title is followed by 'An Epode': i.e. a lyric poem on a serious subject. The poem is commonly dated 1649, to fit Lovelace's second spell in prison; but its recapitulation of the Kentish petition and its reference to the 'Public Faith' make 1642, the period of his first imprisonment, far more likely (see H.A. Margoliouth's review of Wilkinson's edition in *Review of English Studies*, 3, 1927, pp. 93-4).
1-4   not an easy stanza to interpret: to make sense of it, *liberty* should not be treated as a vocative, but as the object of *ask*; *thee* should be taken to refer to Lucasta, who will be 'left for a while another's bride'; and *fancy* should be taken as a verb.
6   *prove*   test, examine
7-8   *Then . . . mine* i.e. then I will confine my free soul to whatever I can possibly call my own.
18   *thorough-shot*   shot through
30   *sovereign salve*   master remedy
37   *Public Faith*   money forcibly borrowed by parliament (and not often repaid).
40   *cozens*   cheats
43   *spring*   source, but continuing the watch-making image of ll. 35-6.
53   *starry wain*   Charles's Wain, Ursa Major.

p.32 *Lucasta's Fan, With a Looking Glass in it*   The fan is made of

97

ostrich feather, with an inset mirror, As well as hiding
its head in the sand and eating anything, the ostrich was
famous for deserting its young in their nest.

1   *Ostrich* Spelt *Eastrich* in the original text.

10   *th' arch of heaven* the rainbow

19   *whenas* when

21   *engine* implement, contrivance
      got'st me the day i.e. triumphed over, with the paradox
      of getting the day over the sun, the ruler of daylight.

25   *shade* image, i.e. reflection in the fan's mirror.

27   *but unto ourselves* except for ourselves

35   *Alexis* Lovelace's name for himself in his poetry.

36   *dress* perhaps playing on *address* too.

p.33 *Lucasta, taking the waters at Tunbridge* The title is followed
by 'Ode'. Compare this poem with *Lucasta at the Bath* in
the *Posthume Poems* volume (p.65). Lucasta's 'taking the
waters' seems to describe both her bathing in the spa and
her drinking its waters. The anatomical conceits relate to
drinking (l.17) and the water that seeps into her vagina (l.9).

p.34 *To My Worthy Friend Mr Peter Lely* Sir Peter Lely (1618-80)
was entered into the Company of Painters at the same
time as Lovelace. There is another poem addressed to him
in *Posthume Poems*, where Lovelace writes

> Now my best Lely let's walk hand in hand
> And smile at this un-understanding land;
> Let them their own dull counterfeits adore,
> Their rainbow-clothes admire, and no more;
> Within one shade of thine more substance is
> Than all their varnished idol-mistresses.
> <div align="right">(<i>Peinture</i>, 101-6)</div>

The portrait of Charles and his son was made at the time
when the King was held prisoner in Hampton Court, where
closely supervised visits from his children were allowed.
Such visits took place in July 1647 and later in the same year.

1   *clouded majesty*   literally so: the background of the portrait shows a cloud-darkened sky behind the Duke of York's head.

3   *bravery*   picked up again in *those brave eyes* in line 20. *Brave* and *bravery* were protean words in the seventeenth century, ranging in meaning from near technical artistic expressions to virtually meaningless clichés of approbation; see Elizabeth Cook's 'The Bravery of Shakespeare's Sonnets', in *Proceedings of the British Academy*, 69, 1983, esp. pp. 191-3.

7-8   *that others...below*   that others, even if they are set at the top of Fortune's wheel, appear below him; *or*, that all others appear to be as far below him as if they were at the bottom of Fortune's wheel and he at the top.

11   *Eaglet*   the King's son, the Duke of York

14   *lightly* playing on *light* as the opposite of *dark* or *heavy*.

15   *passion*   pronounced with three syllables.

20   *Sitters*   the first recorded used of the word in this sense.

21   *speak*   stand for

24   *hieroglyphics*   symbols

25   *typified*   was symbolized

27   *orientally*   from the sense of *orient* as glowing, resplendent. Lovelace is praising Lely's super-realism, which captures the essence as well as the appearance of what he paints.

p.36 *Ellinda's Glove*   In *The Country and the City*, Raymond Williams describes this as 'a strange poem' through which 'we see momentarily more of actual seventeenth-century life than in the poems of retirement' (p.25).

3   *rents*   note the sexual connotations, followed up in *rude possession* in line 5.

7   *alablaster*   alabaster

14-15   *Yet servants...the case*   the minikin is the treble string of the lute. Behind the conceit is the idea that if he may not penetrate her, at the least he ought to be allowed to masturbate her.

p.36 *To Fletcher Revived*   One of the many contributions to the

99

Beaumont and Fletcher Folio, *Comedies and Tragedies*, in 1647. The whole occasion was very much a piece of Royalist propaganda, but, significantly, Lovelace's contribution was one of the most restrained. This poem, unlike many of the others, blames the closing of the theatres not upon the malice of Parliament, but upon the failure of the dramatists of the 1620s and 1630s to follow Fletcher's example of treating vice without giving offence.

11   *flamens*   priests in ancient Rome

18   *signs*   assigns

20   *buskins*   boots traditionally worn by tragic actors.

21-5   *Aetius...Mighty Fool...Valentinian*   references to Fletcher's play *Valentinian*. Later references in the poem are to Beaumont and Fletcher's comedies and tragi-comedies.

29-32   *Not as of old...sob'rer tone*   Alcides is Hercules. Lovelace is probably thinking of Thomas Heywood's play *The Brazen Age* (1613), which has the roaring bull in Act 1, the rock in Act 5, and much roaring by Hercules when he dies at the end of the play.

48   *stews and shores*   brothels and sewers

52   *Minerva*   the goddess of wisdom

60   *austere scarlet*   the Parliamentary censors

70   *the best piece...e'er read*   Wilkinson notes that Correggio's *Mercury teaching Cupid to read*, now in the National Gallery, was formerly in the collection of Charles I.

p.39 *Against the Love of Great Ones*

2   *sainted hate*   i.e. made hate its saint

3   *bands*   the 1649 text has *bonds*

3-4   understand *which* between these two lines to make sense of them.

11   *Ixion* sentenced to perpetual torture and chained to a wheel by Zeus, because of his attempt to win the love of Hera.

12   *gyre*   turning

21   *Semele*   loved by Zeus in his role as god of thunder, and consumed by lightning.

34   *box or gem*   the jewel-box or the jewel which it contains: *thing or show* makes the sexual point more obviously.

48   *bring*   bring to birth

52   *boorein*   peasant woman

63   *a dying lives*   i.e. endure a living death

p.41 *To Althea, From Prison*   The title is followed by 'Song. Set by Dr John Wilson'. According to Anthony Wood, this poem was written during Lovelace's confinement in the Gatehouse in 1642. This was his best known poem, found in at least six seventeenth-century manuscripts: all but one of these reads *birds* rather than *gods* in line 7, but the printed version has *gods*. For a discussion of stanza four, see W. Empson, *Seven Types of Ambiguity*, p.210.

10   *allaying Thames*   Thames water to dilute it.

p.42 *Being Treated, To Ellinda*

1   *corans*   currants

2   *on's*   of us

3   *ells...flutes*   an *ell* is a measure (45 inches), a *flute* is a tall wine-glass.

4   *pasties-mary*   marrow pasties

5   *peason*   peas

6   *widow-ven'son-pie*   Wilkinson explains that the venison pie is widow 'because someone has had a cut out of it already'.

10   *knuckles...deep in*   they would, of course, eat it with their hands.

12   *loin right-worshipful*   sirloin, from a baron of beef.

20   *dam-Rotter*   i.e. Rotterdam. Lovelace spent several years in Holland in the 1640s.

24   *Hans...Kelder*   Hans-in-Kelder means Jack-in-cellar, an unborn child.

32   *beaker pewter*   tin and lead alloy from which beakers were made.

40   *Amadis, Sir Guy and Topas*   three Romance heroes.

p.43 *A Guiltless Lady Imprisoned*   The title is followed by 'Song. Set Mr William Lawes'.

   9   *gyves* fetters

  10   *Are so unto themselves* this means something like 'they cut into themselves'; it might be possible that Lovelace wrote *fo* (=*foe*).

  24   *epithalamies* marriage-songs

  28   *bands* the 1649 text has *bonds*.

p.44 *To his Dear Brother Colonel F.L.*   The brother addressed is Francis (later to be governor of New York) who was in command at Carmarthen until the town was taken by Parliament. The brother mourned, William, died in the battle there in 1644, probably under Francis's command at the time. This poem begins as an imitation of a Latin ode by the Polish poet Casimir Sarbiewski (1595-1640): see J.C. Arens's essay in *Neophilologus*, 47, 1963, pp. 236-9.

p.45 *La Bella Bona Roba*   A *bona roba* is a prostitute. See the debate about the 'modernity' of this poem, between Marius Bewley and Donald Davie, in *Scrutiny*, 16, 1949, pp. 12-19 & 234-41.

   5   *incarnadine* flesh-coloured

  10   *hard hap* ill fortune

  12   *'say* assay, attempt

        keeper's fees the customary payment for the gamekeeper after a successful hunt: shoulders, innards, and horns.

  14   *heart-chasing* with the usual pun on *hart*.

  15   *rascal deer* lean deer

p.46 *The Fair Beggar*

   9   *thrice-bequeathed* i.e. passed down through three generations.

  15   *motions* puppets

p.47 *Amyntor from beyond the Sea to Alexis*   Amyntor is probably Endymion Porter, Alexis is Lovelace. Porter was in exile in Holland in 1647-8. Chloris (l.18) would then be Porter's wife. Dialogue poems were common in seventeenth-century secular and religious poetry.

38   *green-god*   Neptune
44   *his queen*   Amphitrite

p.49 *A Lady with a Falcon on her fist*   The *cousin A.L.* is Anne
Lovelace, to whom Lovelace dedicated the whole volume
of *Lucasta*.
3   *silken clue*   thread of silk
5-6   *The swelling Admiral...Oh Fair*   Wilkinson guesses that
Anne Lovelace's husband, the second Baron Lovelace of
Hurley, was at one time connected with the sea.
22-4   *Falcon's monarchy...nobler is the she*   the falcon is the
name given to the female of the species: the male, a smaller
bird, is called the tercel.

p.50 *Calling Lucasta from her Retirement*
5   *Cimmerian*   gloomy: the Cimerii lived in perpetual night.
17   *owe*   own, possess
21   *alarums*   the 1649 text reads *alarmes*.

p.52 *Aramantha*   This poem is separately advertised on the title
page of *Lucasta*.
10   *weed*   garment
21-4   *washes... bladders... plashes... venom-tempered water...
Mercury*   various cosmetic washes and perfumes.
40   *crisping*   which makes curls
44   *discoloured*   variegated
53   *Heliotropian*   sunflower
56   *loyal golden Mary*   i.e. the marigold
62   *the poor Girl*   the violet
63   *July-flower*   clove pink; gillyflower
73   *contemns*   disdains
109-10   *Making...bull*   Io was metamorphosed into a heifer
by Zeus; Europa was courted by him in the form of a bull.
120 *Cynthia*   the moon
121 *writhelled*   wrinkled
122 *obsequies*   funeral rites

130 *neat*   cattle

132 *hollowed*   Wilkinson emends to *hallowed*, but *hollowed* (=concave) makes good enough sense, and cp. l.250, where he keeps the 1649 text's *hollowed*, but where *hallowed* would fit just as well as here.

138 *fry*   fish

158 *supplied...self-recruit*   i.e. nature keeps replenishing itself: *recruit* had just entered the language, in a number of chiefly military senses, in the 1640s.

226 *posses her round*   pushes her way round

231 *antic*   absurd

240 *anthems*   songs sung by two voices

241 *her breath's*   some 1649 texts have *my breath's*

281 *Paphos*   the city where Venus was worshipped.

291 *cheap*   poor

304 *stripping*   i.e. looting the dead body

327-8 *Hydraphil...Philanact*   the lover of the multitude and the lover of the prince: i.e. puritans and cavaliers.

358 *gust*   taste

367 *humble Crook*   the shepherd's life: *crook* looks forward to the play on bishoprics in l.370.

p.62 *To Lucasta: Her Reserved Looks*
  7-8   *So in one picture...*   describes a picture which, when looked at from different angles, shows either an angel or a devil.

p.63 *Lucasta Laughing*
  15-16   *sinister-handed...doth go*   i.e. like a root which turns the wrong way and grows downward rather than up.

p.64 *Song*
  5   *lawn*   fine linen
  13   *gauderies*   finery
  15   *clinquant*   tinsel

p.64 *Her Muff*   Partridge dates the slang use of this word to mean the female pudend from the late seventeenth-century. This

104

poem puts it back to the 1650s.

1   *deceive*   Wilkinson emends this to *receive*, but the 1659 text makes sense if one relates it to Jacob's deception of his father in order to gain the blessing due to Esau (Genesis 27).

20   *sables upon ermine*   black on white

21   *lay-lovers*   the uninitiated

p.65 *Lucasta at the Bath*

10   *wan*   paleness

26   *blains*   swellings (as in chilblains)

p.67 *The Ant*

1   *husband*   tiller of the soil; head of the household.

10   *Cato*   left the theatre so that the people should not be too embarrassed to call for their naked entertainers. Lovelace implies that, on occasion, he stayed to watch.

14   *fueillemort*   of a faded colour

22   *wain*   wagon

27-8   *Margaret Pie...John Daw*   magpie and jackdaw

34   *maw*   stomach

p.68 *The Snail*   For a discussion of the political implications of this poem, see R.L. Wadsworth's essay in *Modern Language Review*, 65, 1970, pp. 750-60.

13   *preventing*   coming before

18   *Cynthia's*   the moon's

20   *Phoebus*   the sun

31   *cubs of India*   Wilkinson quotes Stephens' description of 'that forraine creature, called by the name of *Su*' which 'shuts up her cubbes in a depending scrip, and so protects them from the Huntsman' (*Satyrical Essayes*, 1615, p.90).

39   *husband*   see the note to line 1 of *The Ant*.

    still within   always at home

52   *fane*   temple

    cupola'd   covered with a dome

55   *eliminat'st*   the OED cites this as the only example of the

word used in the meaning 'to pass the threshold of, come out of': really, in keeping with the wit of the poem, this is only an etymological pun, *eliminate* deriving from the Latin *limen*, 'threshold'.

p.70 *A Loose Saraband*   Lovelace's second poem with this title: see the note on p.96.

6   *vestal*   virginal
8   *wild Canary*   Canary wine
9   *off with*   drink down
     crowned Venice   Venetian goblet
11   *Rhenish*   Rhine wine
13   *milk...assuageth*   i.e. milk always cools lightning.
16   *posset*   a drink composed of hot milk curdled with liquor.
17   *a well wisher*
18   *nag*   Partridge dates the use of this word to mean 'penis' from 1670, but it makes good sense here (picking up the milk/sperm connotations of the previous stanza).
19-20   *cellar...buttery*   the wine cellar as opposed to the place where the wine was stored (continuing the sexual wordplay).
22   *broached*   *broach* means 'to pierce a cask to draw liquor off' and 'to start an argument'.
24   *still...taster*   i.e. Love employs Lovelace to do his tasting for him, to make sure the wine is not sour: with a play on *guest* and *gust*.
32   *amber*   perfume: OED cites from earlier in the century, 'be sure the wines be lusty, high, and full of spirit, and amber'd all...'
39   *October*   OED cites the meaning as 'Ale brewed in October', which it says is 'common in the eighteenth century'. As so often, Lovelace's use antedates the first recorded occurrence by more than fifty years.

p.72 *The Falcon*   For an allegorical reading of this poem, see R.A. Anselment's essay in the *Journal of English & Germanic Philology*, 70, 1971, 404-17. Earl Miner writes that this poem is

the best example he knows of 'a great deal of poetry...
written between 1640 and 1660 in which a political or topical
intent seems as certainly to be meant as to be certainly
difficult or impossible to unravel' (*The Cavalier Mode from
Jonson to Cotton*, p.178). For the battle between the falcon
and the heron, Wilkinson refers to these accounts, from
Turberville's *Book of Falconrie* (1611, p.164) and Wesley's
Maggots (1685, p.10):

> When your Hawke will kill a traine lustily, and boldly,
> then may you goe into the field to finde a wilde Hearon
> at siege, and when you have found her, win as nie to
> her as you can, and goe with your Hawk under the
> wind, where having first loosed her hoode in a readi-
> nesse, as soone as the Hearon leaveth the siege, off with
> her hoode, and let her flee...
> The Custom of the Hearn when she sees the Hawk,
> stooping at her, and no way of escape, is to turn her
> Long Bill upwards, upon which the Hawk not being
> able to stop, runs itself through, and so both often drop
> down dead together.

7 *Bird Imperial* the eagle
8 *pennons* wings; ensigns
10 *cousin-german* first cousin
22 *varvels* rings around the falcon's feet.
29 *helm* hood
31 *the Arabian bird* the phoenix
33 *lose you* lose yourself
34 *sours* i.e. makes them seem sour by comparison.
39 *hinds* servants
42 *epicedium* funeral ode
44 *lanceer* lancer
45 *hut* an old form of *hide*: but Lovelace is probably using
    the verb in a military sense, in keeping with the metaphor
    here. The OED dates from 1652 the meaning 'to place (troops,
    etc.) in huts, esp. for winter quarters'.

46 *halberdier* foot-soldier, armed with a spear.
69 *fries* burns with anger
78 *palisadoes* fence-like fortifications
86 *pounced* the OED dates from 1686 the first use of this word in the sense 'to seize, as a bird of prey, with the pounces or talons'.
87 *stoops* a technical hawking term: to descend swiftly on the prey.
89 *bells* fixed to the falcon's feet.
97 *hobby and musket* kinds of small hawk
99 *lanner and lanneret* a species of falcon, female and male respectively.
100 *banneret* a knight, entitled to carry his own banner onto the battlefield.
102 *boused* a technical term: letting the hawk drink as much as it wants.
104 *various* variegated

p.75 *Love Made in the First Age*
3 *direct Hebrew* the stanza plays on the idea that Hebrew, the original language, is more direct because it is written from right to left: later ages have reversed this, and are therefore backward.
5 *retrograde . . . desire* a strange echo of Claudius's words, 'it is most retrograde to our desire' (*Hamlet* I:ii:115).
24 *suits of trespass* playing on the ideas of law-suits for trespassing on private land and suits of clothes made as a consequence of the Fall.
26 *diapered* patterned
33 *clasp* most 1659 texts read *clap*
54 *zone* literally 'belt', hence the idea of being girded with it.

p.77To *A Lady with child that asked an Old Shirt* The poem is based on the custom of giving an article of clothing to a woman soon to give birth.
4 *to set . . . on fire* alluding to the shirt of Nessus.
13 *nine sempstresses* the Muses

15   *the jolli'st*   Thalia, the muse of comedy: as the eighth muse
she is particularly appropriate to the woman in her eighth
month.

18   *clout*   piece of cloth

p.78 *Cupid Far Gone*

9   *Cybele*   the Greek mother goddess

12   *antipodes*   Partridge dates the usage of this word to mean
the backside only from the nineteenth century, but this is
probably Lovelace's meaning here.

13   *Psyche*   Cupid's lover

14   *quarrels...Mercury*   i.e. engages in controversy with the
most academic of the gods.

18   *Juno*   the queen of heaven

25   *Olympus*   the mountain residence of the gods

27   *Charon*   the ferryman of hell

28   *Argus*   emendation to *Argo* has been suggested, but Lovelace is not likely to have made so elementary an error:
Argus Panoptes is probably intended here. He was the
hundred-eyed guardian of Io, transformed into a peacock
after his death: *rigged* here means 'dressed up'.

29   *Cerberus*   the three-headed dog who guarded the entrance
to hell.

p.79 *A Mock-Song*   *Mock* means both counterfeit and mocking.
For an explication of the references in this poem, see W.
McClung Evans's essay in *Philological Quarterly*, 24, 1945,
pp. 317-28.

7   *Tarquin*   i.e. Charles I

24   *Spent-gorge*   Wilkinson explains this as a quibble on the
'full-gorge' of feeding hawks, and meaning therefore that
'their cut-throats have emptied themselves', and meta-
phorically that the knights have been destroyed. He sees
a possible allusion to Pride's purge in November 1648

26   *hony soit*   the motto of the Order of the Garter.

p.80 *A Fly Caught in a Cobweb*

4   *catch at*   attempt to imitate

9   *toil*   net

10   *keep'st a . . . coil*   keep up a disturbance

14   *quartered*   cut into pieces; lodged.

21   *like him, whose coil*   Zeus's son, Phaeton.

28   *num'rous mess*   a large meal

37   *like pies . . .*   i.e. those large pies in which the birds were placed head downwards.

44   *castle-enemy*   the elephant

p.82 *A Fly About a Glass of Burnt Claret*

7   *cake*   piece of coal

       'tis said   the 1659 text has *is said*.

10   *heaven-crystalline*   'in the Ptolemaic astronomical system, a sphere . . . supposed to exist between the primum mobile and the firmament' (OED): see *P. Lost* 3:482.

12   *Acheron*   a river in Hades

13   *snowball-heart*   the contemporary method of cooling wine: its undertone is the Petrarchan image of the icy lover melted by passion.

18   *Hymen's pine*   Hymen, the god of marriage, often portrayed as a serious youth with a pinewood torch in his hand.

20   *flambeau*   torch

23   *passed*   drunk and voided

25   *vestal*   virgin

29   *chemist*   alchemist

30   *limbeck's bill*   lip of his retort

31-2   *sublimated bowl . . . calcine*   alchemical terms: *sublimate* is to turn into vapour and make solid again, *calcine* is to turn to powder by heating.

40   *Curtius*   when a chasm opened up in the forum in Rome, Mettius Curtius jumped in on horseback, sacrificing himself as the greatest treasure Rome could offer the gods.

43   *the sun's son*   Phaeton

45   *auricular*   little finger (i.e. the one most suited to sticking

in one's ear).

p.84 *Advice to my Best Brother*   For an account of Francis Lovelace,
see the note to *To his Dear Brother Colonel F.L.* (p.102). The
major part of this poem, from line 29, is based on Horace's
ode (II:10) 'Rectius vives, Licini, neque altum'. Wilkinson
calls attention to the possibility that the strange phrase
glassy epithet, in line 4, echoes another Horatian ode (IV:2),
which refers to the way the doomed son of Dedalus gave
his name to the sea he died in. Could Lovelace be thinking
of the North Sea as the Frankish sea?

6   *halcyon's nest*   the kingfisher, who charms the sea into
calmness.

12   *Dione's cradle*   Dione was the mother of Aphrodite, who
came out of the ocean.
Thetis' blankets   Thetis was the mother of Achilles: perhaps
Lovelace is thinking of her prophecy to her son that he
would either live a glorious but short life, or live a long
inglorious one.

25   *Ixion's wheel*   see the note to l.11 of *Against the Love of Great
Ones* (p.100).

28   *antic*   grotesque, with a play on *antique* too.

29   *golden mean*   Horace's *aurea mediocritas*: the avoidance of
excess.

30   *cot*   cottage
entailed   passed from heir to heir, with none having the
right to dispose of it.

34   *looking-glass and feather*   see *Lucasta's Fan* (p.97)

35   *which larks would play with*   it was falconers' practice to
dazzle a lark with a piece of scarlet cloth.

44   *declines to fall*   i.e. falls down (not *declines* in the sense of
refuses).

46   *batters and scales*   principally a siege metaphor, assaulting
and then scaling the walls; but also the sense of chipping
at the surface.

47   *breast of proof*   a breast capable of standing the test: this

111

continues the military imagery, *proof* having originally described armour – *armour of proof* was a common phrase.

53   *Aelos*   the god of winds
54   *Zephyrus...Boreas*   west wind and north wind
55   *false sequel, solecism*   false logic, an error
58   *Apollo*   the god of poetry and archery (hence the bow and harp).

p.86 *To Dr F.B. On his Book of Chess*   Lovelace's is one of three poems commending *The Royall Game of Chesse-Play*, published in 1656. There are minor, but unimportant, differences between the text of the poem and the 1659 text, which is printed here. The book's subtitle is of some interest: it begins *Sometimes The Recreation of the late King, with many of the Nobility...*

2   *Fox and Geese*   a popular game
8   *cluttered*   crowded together

p.86 *On Sannazar's being honoured...*   Jacopo Sannazaro (1458-1530) was rewarded for the following hexastich (this is Lovelace's translation):

> In Adriatic waves when Neptune saw,
> The city stand, and give the seas a law,
> Now i' th' Tarpeian towers Jove rival me,
> And Mars his walls impregnable, said he;
> Let seas to Tiber yield, view both their odds,
> You'll grant that built by men, but this by gods.

For the dating of this poem in September 1656, see E.E. Duncan-Jones, 'Two Allusions in Lovelace's Poems', in *Modern Language Review*, 51, 1956, pp. 407-9.

1   *a blithe prince*   Louis XI of France, who rewarded a man who had fed him with radishes when he had been in exile.
4   *Maid of Meurs*   a Dutch girl who was supposed to have lived many years without food.
5   *St Mark*   traditionally associated with Venice.
11   *Lepanto*   when Venice defeated the Turkish fleet in 1572.

13　*Candie*　the Turkish siege of Candia, defended by the Venetians, begun in 1645, was still going on when Lovelace wrote the poem.

14　*half-half moon*　the Turkish crescent.

19　*Augustus*　the emperor who presided over the great age of Roman poetry.

24　*zany*　play the fool with

32　*sons of Phoebus*　the poets

34　*crown*　i.e. the coin, not the laurel wreath.

43　*Olio*　a dish containing a variety of ingredients: a hotch-potch.

47　*sack*　wine
　　drolled　jested

50　*his man's curse*　i.e. his serving-man, who felt he should have been given it.

51　*bossed*　ornamented
　　two to none　i.e. so certain that it's no bet.

59-60　*Diogenes . . . sweet a club*　Diogenes was the Greek Cynic philosopher who chose to live in a tub. Line 60 seems to mean something like: 'However much he scorned them, they refused to be offended'.

64　*young Lovelace*　in Fletcher's *The Scornful Lady*, the last play to be presented at court before the civil war, a character named Loveless promises to dress all his servants in satin if his plans prosper.

78　*fanes*　temples

87　*Aretine*　notorious for his obscene poems which accompanied Romano's pornographic drawings.

102　*Berenice's hair*　her hair was so beautiful that it became an heavenly constellation.

103　*Cassiopeia's chair*　'That starred Ethiop queen' who was set as a constellation in the heavens: its shape is that of a chair.

108　*the last dove*　see Genesis 8:12

116　*sad boon*　solemn request for a favour

117　*Macaroon*　buffoon

113

119 *train-band*   trained company of citizen soldiers in London.

123 *contract*   a marriage contract

128-31   Lovelace presses the parallel between the Grub-street poets' writings and their desire for food: *sippets* means both small pieces of toast and fragments of verse; *minced* means both mutilated and affected (as in *mincing*).

132 *knots*   alludes to the marriage being celebrated and plays on the sense of the word as 'an intricate flourish of the pen'.

134 *drills*   mandrills, monkeys

135 *maw*   belly

142 *pismire*   ant

143 *Alcides*   Hercules

152 *Nimrod*   see Genesis 10:8-10

161 *Helicon*   the fountain of the muses.
       naumachy   a sea battle

162 *Parnassus*   the mountain seat of the muses.

163 *Minerva*   the goddess of wisdom

168 *Decemviri*   ten men who drew up the laws of Rome.

172 *golden tripod*   three-legged stool, similar to the one from which the Delphic oracle was delivered.

182-3   *Envy . . . their right*   added in the margin is a reference to the origin of these lines, in Ovid's Elegy 15: but here Lovelace is quoting verbatim from Ben Jonson's rendering of them in *The Poetaster*, where the words are put in Ovid's mouth (1:1:166-7). The play was much in Lovelace's mind: see line 224.

186 *unweeting*   without realizing

190 *dear uncle*   George Sandys (1578-1644), Archbishop of York, was Lovelace's great uncle, who translated Ovid's *Metamorphoses*, and wrote paraphrases of the Psalms and hymns of the Old Testament.

196 *Wenman*   spelt *Waynman*: probably Sir Thomas Wenman (1596-1665), a very minor poet.

198 *Falkland*   Lucius Cary (1610-43), the addressee of Jonson's great Cary-Morison ode: patron of poets and poet himself.

210 *all-in all-in*   the final peal of bells before the service begins

This is Wilkinson's emendation: the 1659 text has *all-in* only once.

212 *mercer*   a dealer in fabrics

214 *ell*   a measure: 45 inches.

216 *drawer*   tapster

rack   playing on the two senses, of stretching on a rack, and drawing off wine from the lees.

218 *bar-maid*   antedates the OED's first recorded use of the word by more than an hundred years.

219 *posset*   see note to line 16 of *A Loose Saraband* (p.106).

224 *Crispinus*   character in *The Poetaster*.

226-30   Imitating Jonson's 'apologetical Dialogue' added to the folio text of *The Poetaster*: to *rive a quill* is to split a pen open.

234 *Father Ben*   Ben Jonson

249 *one Sappho*   Wilkinson guesses that the one woman poet excepted from Lovelace's diatribe is Katherine Phillips. Equally, of course, the line can be read ironically, making her the worst of all.

252 *Clarissimi*   Venetian grandees

261 *For it is . . . write*   from Juvenal (1:30) 'Difficile est satiram non scribere'.

115

Index of first lines

117

Fyfield*Books*

"The Fyfield Books series provides an admirable service in publishing good inexpensive selections from the works of interesting but neglected poets"
– British Book News

THOMAS LOVELL BEDDOES (1803-49)
Selected Poems
edited by Judith Higgens

THE BRONTË SISTERS
Selected Poems
edited by Stevie Davies

ELIZABETH BARRETT BROWNING (1806-61)
Selected Poems
edited by Malcolm Hicks

THOMAS CAMPION (1567-1620)
Ayres and Observations
edited by Joan Hart

GEORGE CHAPMAN (?1559-1634)
Selected Poems
edited by Eirean Wain

THOMAS CHATTERTON (1752-70)
Selected Poems
edited by Grevel Lindop

CHARLES COTTON (1630-87)
Selected Poems
edited by Ken Robinson

WILLIAM COWPER (1731-1800)
Selected Poems
edited by Nick Rhodes

GEORGE CRABBE (1754-1832)
Selected Poems
edited by Jem Poster

RICHARD CRASHAW (1612/13-49)
Selected Poems
edited by Michael Cayley

MICHAEL DRAYTON (1563-1631)
Selected Poems
edited by Vivian Thomas

GEORGE GASCOIGNE (1530-77)
The Green Knight:
selected poems and prose
edited by Roger Pooley

JOHN GAY (1685-1732)
Selected Poems
edited by Marcus Walsh

JOHN GOWER (1330-1408)
Selected Poetry
edited by Carole Weinberg

THOMAS GRAY (1716-71)
Selected Poems
edited by John Heath-Stubbs

ROBERT HENRYSON (1425?-1508?)
Selected Poems
edited by W.R.J. Barron

ROBERT HERRICK (1591-1674)
Selected Poems
edited by David Jesson-Dibley

THOMAS HOCCLEVE (?1348-1430)
Selected Poems
edited by Bernard O'Donoghue

BEN JONSON (1572-1637)
Epigrams & The Forest
edited by Richard Dutton

WALTER SAVAGE LANDOR (1775-1864)
Selected Poems and Prose
edited by Keith Hanley

ANDREW MARVELL (1621-78)
Selected Poems
edited by Bill Hutchings

GEORGE MEREDITH (1828-1909)
Selected Poems
edited by Keith Hanley

CHARLES OF ORLEANS (1394-1465)
Selected Poems
edited by Sally Purcell

SIR WALTER RALEGH (?1554-1618)
Selected Writings
edited by Gerald Hammond

JOHN WILMOT, EARL OF ROCHESTER
(1648-80)
The Debt to Pleasure
edited by John Adlard

CHRISTINA ROSSETTI (1830-94)
Selected Poems
edited by C.H. Sisson

SIR PHILIP SIDNEY (1554-86)
Selected Poetry and Prose
edited by Richard Dutton

JOHN SKELTON (1460-1529)
Selected Poems
edited by Gerald Hammond

CHRISTOPHER SMART (1722-71)
Selected Poems
edited by Marcus Walsh

DONALD STANFORD (editor)
Three Poets of the Rhymers' Club:
Lionel Johnson, Ernest Dowson,
John Davidson

HENRY HOWARD, EARL OF SURREY
(1517-47)
Selected Poems
edited by Dennis Keene

JONATHAN SWIFT (1667-1745)
Selected Poems
edited by C.H. Sisson

ALGERNON CHARLES SWINBURNE
(1837-1909)
Selected Poems
edited by L.M. Findlay

ARTHUR SYMONS (1865-1945)
Selected Writings
edited by R.V. Holdsworth

THOMAS TRAHERNE (?1637-74)
Selected Writings
edited by Dick Davis

HENRY VAUGHAN (1622-95)
Selected Poems
edited by Robert B. Shaw

ANNE FINCH, COUNTESS OF WINCHILSEA
(1661-1720)
Selected Poems
edited by Denys Thompson

EDWARD YOUNG (1683-1765)
Selected Poems
edited by Brian Hepworth

"Carcanet are doing an excellent job in this series: the editions are labours of love, not just commercial enterprises. I hope they are familiar to all readers and teachers of literature." – *Times Literary Supplement*